MW00675601

TAPESTRIES

INSPIRATIONAL

MURIEL R. GREEN

Tapestries by Muriel Ratteray Green
Copyright © 2007 by Muriel Ratteray Green
All Rights reserved.
ISBN: 1-59755-096-5

Published By: ADVANTAGE BOOKS™
                 www.advbooks.com

This book and parts therefore may not be reproduced in any form, stored in any retrieval system or transmitted in any form by any means (electronic, mechanical, photocopy, recording or otherwise) without prior written permission of the author, except as provided by the United States of America copyright law.

Library of Congress Control Number: 2007921843

Cover Design by Pat Theriault
Interior Design by David Janiczek

First Printing: October 2007
07 08 09 10 11 12 13 10 9 8 7 6 5 4 3 2
Printed in the United States of America

Dedication

Dedicated to my beloved Parents: Charles and Joanna Ratteray

To my early spiritual Guides: Rev. and Mrs. Williams Ellison and Bishop Roderick Caesar, Sr.

My current spiritual leaders: Bishop Roderick Caesar, Jr. and Pastor Beverly Caesar and Pastor Allan P. Plummer

Acknowledgements

This is the story of my life, beginning from my earliest recollection up until this present time.

Acknowledgements of my Medical Doctors for their care and concern they afforded me during my illness: Dr. Walter Johnson, Neuro-Surgeon, Dr. Richard Swanson, Neuro-Surgeon, Dr. Geigerich, Endocrinologist, Dr.C. Resta, Endocrinologist, Dr. G. Gomes, Internist

Muriel Ratteray Green

Table of Contents

Introduction

I always wanted to put my life's story down on paper, and in the beginning of 1990, I began scribbling notes on pieces of paper. I would misplace and lose these scribblings; and sometimes give up, not writing anything else for months at a time. Being a reserved quiet type of person, I would argue with myself as to who would want to read about the life of one so unobtrusive as myself. Why would anyone want to read such uninteresting triviotics, as my experiences appeared to be to me as I embarked on this journey? Which is really what it is; from the time of my birth up until the present days.

But it occurred to me as I started to put the pieces of my life's events together, that those outside my immediate sphere might be intrigued with the events of my life. The story emerges in the late 1920's. The beginning of which, almost as soon as I was able to walk and talk were very vivid to me.

Then it dawned on me, that I have a lot to share with the outside world. Yes I became bold enough to believe that the generations born in the 1950's the 1960's, and the 1970's would be interested in my babblings. After all I am a child of the Depression days. Lived through World War II, the Korean War, and the Viet Nam Confrontation. After raising five children, I decided to go into nursing at the age of forty-three.

Nursing is not for a quiet unassuming person. How could a timid young negro woman (as we were called negroes in earlier days) brought up in a very straight laced family setting, married to the first man in her life, who's cheeks would flush, if a young man's eyes lingered too long on hers; accomplish such a feat. With no ill references to present day Nursing Schools, I must shed light on this matter. Back then in the 1960's and 1970's Nursing Schools were not mainly reading, researching and sitting in study groups tutoring each other. We had no study buddies who we could call on to help you through a difficult assignment. We were thrown out on an active Medical Surgical floor, the second week of Nursing School with our other instructor close at our heels to shout and scream the students into humiliation in front of their peers and sick patients, if we made one simple blunder. I understood later on that these tactics were employed so as to weed out the wary, the insecure, the insincere and the undedicated.

I scribbled many incidences down, folded them up between the pages of my beloved Bible and trusty dictionary. It was not until the late part of 1992 and the early part of 1993 that I realized that my life had taken so many shapes and turns, that the telling of my experiences would be beneficial to someone else. You see I have met up with some very harrowing fight or flight situations, some of which I was not able to do either. At one point in my life I became very numb and almost a mental cripple, but I overcame these life's traumas.

In another instance I became very ill. Almost overnight my eyesight began to diminish. This was a symptom of a much greater medical problem. How could I handle such a ghostly ogre with its ugly clutching fingers? My independence was threatened, my children were frightened and my faith in God was challenged. Would I waver? Did I succumb to any of these forces around; who advised; just give up gracefully, make out your will, and get your house in order. Well friends all this advice floated over my head. I was not ever going to gracefully give up, had no will to make out, and my house was always kept in order.

Now, Thank the Lord, I am able to move about on my own steam, cook for myself and family, attend my beloved church as often as I can, because my dear Lord and Savior Jesus Christ, had been my bulwark on the stormy seas of life. I do have quite a few lines to write down. Don't be curious just read the ensuing chapters.

I sit here on my faded blue and beige plaid couch, scratched and torn by my loving cat "Blanchie", with the tapestry of my life spread out over my knees. I know now with a certainty you will be touched and moved by these spirited episodes in my existence. The beautiful colorful ribbons weaving in and out of my Tapestry, creating the Design of my life tells me that the time will be well spent for whoever will dare to turn these pages.

CHAPTER ONE

Early Childhood

All tales have their beginnings. Mine has a quiet simple beginning. I'll begin then quite simply. I was born Muriel Ratteray on Fox Street in an apartment building in the Bronx, N.Y. It was a mixed neighborhood but at that time so I am told that mostly the Jewish family lived in that area. So I understand that Mama and Daddy, Jeanie and myself were the only coloreds as we were called then for blocks around. My parents were superintendents of the Apartment house that we lived in. We lived on the ground floor of the five-story building they took care of. Fire escapes adorned the front, and green and white awnings were drawn over the windows to keep out the afternoon sun. The "Sun" with the Jewish people was always a conversational opener. "Nice and Sunny today," they would greet each other. "Sit on the corner you'll get more sun." So they lined up their folding chairs on the corner to drink in the sun. "But don't let the sun in the apartment," they admonished each other. "It'll fade the drapes & upholstery." So they would sink down in their chairs and throw their heads back and reminisce on the former days when they were able to spend the winter months in Florida. Up in the Bronx in those early days, the streets were safe and serene, and the beach chairs come out every April to welcome the spring. Mothers waited on the stoops of their apartment buildings for their children chasing each other home from school.

I saw the first light of day on the fourth day of January 1928. Mama was burdened with carrying me for such a lengthy nine months. I was ten and a half lbs, long arms and legs and a big head. I had big blue green eyes and a bushy head of hair. My parents, Charles and Joanna Ratteray were light skinned colored folks. Somewhere in both their family lines was the mixing of white blood. There were light eyes on both sides of our family but Mama and Daddy both had brown eyes. Jeanie had black button eyes and here I arrived with light eyes.

My parents Charles and Joanna were good people with honest business inclinations. As early as I can remember, Daddy had a little sign he hand printed himself. It simply stated "Come on Business, Be on Business, Leave on Business." Daddy kept the building where we lived spotless; sweeping and mopping everyday after 12:00 o'clock noon because he drove a taxi every night until 5:00 AM every day six days a week. Mama polished all the doorknobs and mailboxes. She kept the lobby mirrors and brass frames sparkling. She kept tract of all the tenant's complaints and collected the rents for the owners of the building. She was a very busy young lady taking care of her family that included her two baby girls who were just about two and a half years apart. How did these two young immigrants manage just up from their beautiful native Island of Bermuda? The both of them with their soft British accent and straight laced English customs. They brought with them the willingness and eagerness to learn new and better approaches to life, & the determination to fit in their new American Home. Charles took out citizenship papers almost immediately and the both of them read every book and newspaper available.

Mama said Daddy was a handsome man. Tall and thin with a straight narrow nose and thin lips. Mama was tall and regal, not pretty as she admitted but carried a stately air. My memory serves me back as far as my second year. Believe it or not those arched back windows, looking out into the fenced backyard is still etched in my earliest recollections.

Jeanie had extra long legs like her Mama and Daddy; always running and jumping like a bunny rabbit so they said. Her one sport which she loved best of all, was spring jumping on Mama's big quilted bed. I sat on the foot of the bed one afternoon getting a free ride. Jeanie was not five years old and I had just made my second birthday but this is one of my most vivid memories. Mama was peeling potatoes as always for the lamb stew. She let us sit on the bed next to the old time Emerson radio with the music turned down low. Jeanie leaned over the foot railing, and fingered the dials until the music came in booming. It was a resounding prelude to an afternoon mystery story. She bounced off the bed and took me with her and we both landed between the wall and the bed with the covers pulled over us. I also remember the episode with the yellow spring roll up shade, these window shades fascinated Jeanie to no end. She was never satisfied watching someone perform a certain function of sorts, she had to try it for herself. These shades would not go up and down if you gently pulled on them, you had to jerk them down and let go quickly, then they would slide up, halfway up to the window. Jeanie with her curious black eyes, decided she would experiment when Mama was busy at the sink basin in the kitchen. She pulled the shade down towards the floor and forgot to let go. The shade jumped out of its brackets, pierced her scalp and she ran wailing and bloody to Mama. Mama gave her instant first aid to wounded scalp and backside and that was the end of that.

These are the tidbits of my memories. They are not world shaking but are part of the Tapestry of my life. My little girl days with Mama, Daddy, and Jeanie; the neighborhood and the people. The Jewish people especially. Oh! the questions that these inquisitive folk asked. So curious they were; not in an aloof kind of way, but friendly, and because they really wanted to know. That was their cultural make-up to know that is how the Jewish people managed to survive thrive and prosper. Because they were always in the "know." I knew nothing about discrimination during those early days of my life, although I know it was prevalent all over America during the early 1930's. These people said we were colored and we said nothing. But of course I learned differently later on in life, I have to tell the story the way it really was way back then. When we went to the butchers on the avenue we bought lamb and whole feathered chicken. We always got a soup bone with a little meat left on. All the kids played in the sawdust on the butcher's floor. Next door to the Butcher's was the Bakery. You could buy sweet buns, two for five cents, a seeded rye bread for seven cents and a fat pumpernickel for nine cents. And oh! how the sweet aromas from the warm fresh dough pervaded the air in the streets. And how can I not remember the Jewish Deli with the brown pickled jugs sitting high on the marbled counters. My chin hardly reached the top, but there was always a sliver of roast beef held out to me when Daddy went in to get salami for weekend treats.

Ah yes! these are my early girlhood days. I can now see the overhead "el" train, running along Westchester Avenue, casting shadows on the ground below. Mama, Jeanie, and I would walk along the Avenue in anticipation of Woolworth Dept. Store. Who can forget those early five and dime stores, when almost everything actually could be bought for such a small price or maybe a few pennies more. Always the first stop for Jeanie and I was to the back of the store to watch the gold fish swim in their square glass tanks; and also to watch the yellow and green canaries hopping on their perches, flipping their captive wings in their cages. Mama's first stop was always at the sewing counter where she bought little black and white spools of thread and black elastic to hold up Daddy's shirt sleeves. There were marbles and jacks and tiny tin soldiers for the boys in the toy department. There were all kinds of stuffed dolls & spinning tops. There were huge "Cut out" dolls and coloring books and all for a nickel or a dime. Oh so much to see and all in one store. We usually went once a week with as little as a twenty-five cent piece between Jeanie & I and we were the two happiest children alive, imaginable at the time.

My kindergarten days certainly are vivid ones. I remember my green and white candy striped dress with the wide Peter Pan collar and the black patent lace up boots with white stockings. We lined up in the schoolyard inside the yellow lines. Mama would remove my knitted cap, once on line, shove it down into her deep coat pocket, unbraid and braid over my thick black braids. She did this every morning when standing on line with me waiting for my class to move along. Jeanie was in another class, and the girls and boys were much stronger and taller and did not need their Mama's so close at hand. I know now that Mama wanted to remain with me a little longer so she could survey the other kids in case they shoved or pushed her Mimsie. Yes, that was I, her little Mimsie, a shy little girl with thick black braids and big questioning eyes. I was always ready to cry on school mornings and yearned to cling to Mama and pretend bravery. I would stand in line and wave to Mama when the bell rang and the line moved forward towards the doors and up the steel staircase.

School also had a distinct odor that never will be forgotten. Every September when summer days fade the poignant memory comes back to me. The unique smell of new writing pads, pencil boxes and erasers will always be in my mind. I can't forget the cafeteria on the street floor. We sat on long grey benches and tables. We drank out of dented tin cups, but the creamy milk was the coldest and the tastiest ever. I soon learned to enjoy kindergarten days and especially my teacher Miss Karen. She had long golden shiny hair and she sang like a bird or I thought as much. Miss Karen drew the best from me. She encouraged a shy little girl to sing and recite and always hugged me warmly against her frilly collars when I did well. She taught us group games as well as the alphabet. She taught us to laugh and sing; to clap our hands and stamp our feet to the tunes coming from the old grand piano standing in the corner of the kindergarten room. We folded our hands and sat tall in our seats. We only waved frantically when we had to "leave the room" and couldn't hold it any longer and usually by that time it was too late.

Being picked to be a monitor was the best thing to happen to a first grader. This meant standing at the head of the line, hands straight down at your sides and head held high as teacher called out the rows to the clothing closet. No candy or chewing gum in sight after the bell rang. Anyone caught with his mouth full would have to wear the pink or green glob on his forehead until dismissal time.

Jeanie was in two grades ahead of me, somewhere down the long corridor on the second floor. Everyone in her class including Jeanie seemed so tall. Her third grade teacher was named Miss Franklyn and oh so ugly I thought as compared to Miss Spades my first grade teacher. Mama brought us home from school every afternoon through the Union Ave. Markets. Here she bought tomatoes and string beans from the outdoor stands. Cheese and eggs from the Kosher on 161st Street and seeded rye bread from Cushman's. Now we were loaded down and Mama usually had two shopping bags full, one in each hand; and Jeanie and I with our books in one arm would hold on to the handles of the shopping bags making our way home to the apartment.

Mama was tall then, a stately lady. Her skirts would swish and sway halfway between her knees and ankles. Sometimes I tried to match her steps, but I had to hop and skip to keep up with her stride. These are unforgettable days of my early girlhood. Sometimes the memories drift back to me as sweet smelling aromas. I can smilingly recall Mama's lamb stew this instant. I had always been sensitive to aromas. She always put big chunks of carrots and parsnips in with pink pieces of tender lamb. Little golden balls of dough floated on top. Where did Mama learn such an art? We never had to be coaxed to eat sitting in front of such a fare. After Daddy said the grace the next thing was silence while we cleaned our plates with big chunks of rye seeded bread. Thank God I have never seen a hungry day even though we lived through the depression days. Daddy knew how to earn a dollar and Mama knew how to stretch it six different ways. Daddy was also an English Tailor by trade. He could measure you from neck to knee and present you with a Tailor made suit, dress, pair of pants coat or jacket, whatever you ordered in a matter of one week. Daddy was a very busy man, always working so Mama did not have to go out to the white folks' houses to cook or clean. When he wasn't attending to the apartment building in which we lived he was either Tailoring or driving his Taxi. He had a huge singer sewing machine in the corner of their bedroom. Sometimes I heard it zooming at night when he was filling his orders. We were far from rich; we had sufficient and we were contented and thankful for what we had.

I also remember the winter days back then in the 1930's. The days seemed so much colder then. I remember my brown Teddy Bear coat and my muffler to match. We did not dress for style but for warmth. Mama would wrap Jeanie and I up in heavy plaid scarves when it was especially chilly and stand us up in the sun because as she said the sun was good to kill cold germs. I know now that Mama was a wise lady and had the best brain in the world even though she never earned a diploma from any institution of higher learning.

We had toys and games and "cut out dolls." But my best-loved toy of all was my Shirley Temple cut out doll, hanging outside our closet door. Every now and then Mama would buy a new outfit for my Shirley Temple doll in Woolworth's Store. They sold her outfits in 10-cent books where you cut out her latest party dresses, pleated shirts, and white ruffled blouses with the little tabs folded over the shoulders that you place on the cut out doll. Another passion of mine was drawing and Mama saw to it that I always had a box of crayons, ten for a nickel.

These early days of my childhood are to me beautiful threads of different colors. Intricately woven starting in the center of my being. Here the colors are warm and bright. The design not so distinct at first, like the beginning of a tapestry with the needle of life going in and out the material. The underside of the design might be unusual and vague but turning over the material you will see the beginning of a beautiful pattern, created by a master weaver and in time the design will be much clearer to all those who gaze on it.

By the time I reached seven years old, we made three different moves in the Bronx. We never not stayed too long in each apartment because the next move was to "better." When we left Westchester Ave in the Bronx we left the Building Super's job. The next few moves were from black-bellied stove flats to steam heated apartments with silver painted radiators. Now at this point in time Daddy no longer cared for the apartment buildings we lived in nor was he driving a taxi at night, but he found a job as a "Red Cap" working in the New York Central Railroad System. I was very proud of my Daddy the first time I saw him dressed in his snazzy grey and red uniform. In the summer time Mama would take Jeanie and I on the subway to 42nd Street to meet Daddy on "Pay Day." He would take us around the corner from where he worked to the "Greasy Spoon" where he would order a Spanish Omelet Or Western Omelet for each of us. We had our choice and I always picked the Western Omelet. The green peppers in the yellow egg always looked so appetizing in the pictures over the steaming grill. Mama always sat demurely by with her mug of hot tea and buttered corn muffin. I often wondered why she didn't want something else besides tea and muffins. Daddy always topped the treat with a little glass dish of rice pudding for each of us. Then we would start back home on the train to the Bronx before the rush hour.

Playing house on the fire escape was another adventure that only the children reared in the 1930s or 1940s can remember. Especially on a warm summer's evening. Mama would lean forward from the window next to the fire escape to keep an eye on us. We sipped cool lemonade through glass straws while the clotheslines flipped and flapped their ghostly linens in the cool breeze. Only a few whites were left in the neighborhoods now, they were gradually moving out to Long Island, or upstate New York. The rent was cheap for us; and for twenty five or thirty five dollars a month you had four or five nice rooms with running water, heat, electricity, plenty of neighbors and a candy store on every corner.

Here Daddy saw his opportunity. Folks say they were real hard days. Oh yes they were. It was hard during the depression days. But I watched my Mama and Daddy make their way through that era with very little to go on but their mother wit, their two little girls and a deep abiding faith in God. Yes sir! Daddy saw an opportunity. He saw a tiny little vacant store, wedged between the corner candy store and the Barber Shop at 833 East 167th Street and he opened up a Tailor Shop on those premises. I can still see the big bold black and gold letter painted across the windows of that little shop. "Tailoring for Gents and Ladies," it said. "Cleaning and Steam Pressing done on the Premises."

That year Jeanie and I learned a lot. We became inseparable. Mama made it known we were not to go anywhere without the other. We could not play out in front of the stoop anymore unless we were under the watchful eye of Mama. We were little girls she used to say, "My little girls and I don't want anything to happen to either of you." I did not understand then the fear in Mama's voice, but I heard the whispers between Mrs. Macron the lady in the next apartment. Mama told the whole story to Daddy in hushed tones when he came home from work one evening. He agreed they couldn't play outside by themselves anymore. No more ball and jacks on the stoop below while Mama busied herself in the kitchen. No more jump rope on early Saturday mornings while Mama hung out the wash on the back bedroom clotheslines. Why? I wondered. It was because little Ethel in the next building was missing for a whole week, was found with a huge wound in her head and covered over with a stack of newspaper behind some dented trash cans. Such a sorry happening. Who could do such a hideous thing to such a pretty little girl? Everyone became cautious and suspicious.

Ethel was laid out in a pretty white lace dress and lace gloves. Her little caramel colored arms was showing under the lace puffed sleeves. I dared not look at her face but Jeanie said her lips were purple and drooped in the corners. I thought long and hard. How could that be? Ethel had rosy red lips. She was always laughing and bouncy, and oh so friendly with everyone. Who would want to hurt such a friendly little girl? In the dimly lit living room where Ethel was laid out in a white and grey box were two tall candles lit, one at each end of the box. They said she was lying in a casket. I never saw so many flowers at one time in one place where my little play friend was dead. This was my first encounter with death. The room had an unusual pungent odor. Mama said they were burning incense. I did not want to get to close to Ethel in the casket. I held onto Jeanie's hand tightly and Mama spoke quietly to Ethel's mother and the shadowy people in the room. Then soon we made our way out to the next building and our apartment. From then on Jeanie and I were really inseparable by choice.

Daddy's Tailor Shop did good business. He was a sharp businessman and he knew how to make his business grow. Mama opened the shop everyday for Daddy after giving us our lunch and taking us back to school. Then she would lock up the shop and hurry over to the school and bring us back to the shop. There we would stay and do our homework, while Mama took in the orders and did little mending jobs for Daddy. Mama had a very pleasing personality and was a great asset to Daddy's business. Daddy would come home in the evening and work in his shop, cleaning and pressing and running his sewing machine. In between times, Mama would dart up the street to the apartment and bring Daddy back a tasty dish of something appetizing. He also had his hot glass of tea made on the little electric burner he had in the back of the shop. I don't know how but their routine seemed to work out fine for them, Mama was his right hand man. She would bring us back to the apartment where our plates were waiting for us. Daddy would finish up at the shop and come home in time to listen to the sports and boxing bouts on the radio. Daddy kept his Tailor shop until being rationed; he was not allowed enough oil to run his steam-pressing machine.

I also remember the great rolls of wrapping paper Daddy kept on the Tailor Shop counter to wrap the neatly pressed suits and pants. Jeanie and I always thought we were the first kids ever to use brown wrapping paper to cover our schoolbooks. Daddy would get out his measuring stick and rule out three lines on the front covers of each book. We would print in our best lettering; Spelling, or Arithmetic or whatever the book was, and on the next line we would print the classroom and the name of the teacher.

We had a little wirehaired Fox Terrier dog, which we named Pokey. Mama would take him down the street to the Tailor Shop and put him on a leash outside the shop, and their he would stay until Mama brought Jeanie and I home from school. He would bark and yelp at all the kinds as they hopped on their way home from school, but when he saw Jeanie and I he gave us such outrageous greetings with stamping and panting, and wildly wagging his little nub of a tail. But poor little Pokey met a bitter end one day when he got lose from us. One day when we were going home up the stairs to the apartment, He bounded back down the stairs and we could not find him anywhere in the streets. After two days some young teenage boys discovered his cold stiff little body up on the roof of our building. He had eaten some meat bait put up on the roof to catch mice and little Pokey did not know the difference. Daddy gave the boys twenty-five cents to wrap him in newspaper and dispose of his little body in the trashcans for us. We looked forward to the summer months when school was out. Our block in the Bronx was one of the few that were shut off to traffic. For six weeks all the children in the surrounding area could romp and jump and play games from early morning until four thirty or five in the afternoon, when the Parks' department people put the games and jump ropes away in their truck and left the area. We hopped the potsy boxes trying not to step on the lines. We jumped "Double Dutch rope, chanting "High Water Low Water," "My mother, your mother lives across the way, three sixteen, East Broadway." "Every night they have a fight, and this is what they say." Then every one had their own little catchy verses that they sang while they turned the ropes in a frenzy to call you "OUT."

There were skateboards. Homemade skateboards. Yes made right on your front stoop with nails and woods collected from the neighborhood vegetable store crates. Such a skateboard could hardly be found in a Dept store back then, the boys and girls made them themselves. Hammering them together with nails from the wooden crates after breaking them apart. And Jeanie made herself her own skateboard. She had salvaged some parts of a crate that the older kids had left outside the Tailor Shop. She deliberately broke apart her old pair of skates, found some nails in Daddy's toolbox under his bed and rigged a skateboard. I marveled as I watched her girlish fingers become so adept at such an undertaking. It appeared to my thinking that there was nothing that my older sister could not do. She no longer wanted to play house with our dolls and dress them up. But my greatest worry was that she might displease daddy when he discovered this contraption. Jeanie was a little older than I, so I comforted myself in the fact that she knew what she was doing. I realize now as I look back on those days, that Mama and Daddy both knew that Jeanie was making a skateboard outside the Tailor Shop on those warm summer mornings when we were playing out front, under their watchful eyes.

We were always under their watchful eyes. If we ran up to the other end of the block Mama would step out of the shop and stand with folded arms until we skipped back. Then she would say quietly but sternly, pointing her finger at our noses, "Don't forget no further than the Corner." Summer days came and left swiftly. So grew the tapestry of our lives. Beautiful threads weaving in and out, creating a design on the underside, sometimes quite indistinctive. The threads repeating themselves, going in and out so that the outside could keep its design.

Mama was a very friendly lady. She knew and spoke to everyone on our block. About this time I recall Mama to be in her late thirties'. Her pompadour was sprinkled prematurely with white. Her skin was a soft peachy cream color. I learned in later years Mama was what some folks called "High Yellow." She talked with everyone and told about her Lord & Savior Jesus Christ, and her "Old Time Religion." She loved God with all her heart, showed it in all of her ways and could sing his praises whenever the spirit moved her. Mama said she got saved in her native Bermuda when just a little girl when some Missionary preachers came from the U.S. and held tent meetings there. Mama could also recite poetry and she wrote long notes to our teachers describing our illnesses whenever we were absent from school. I observed later that these notes were hardly every really read by my teachers but were filed away in a yellow manila envelope in the teacher's second drawer.

Mama loved all children, and everyone's child was also her little girl or boy. She used to baby sit for some of the Mother's on the block and would keep them on short notice. A lady I remember so well named Sis. Beaman from the church where we went to have a cute little girl named Valerie. She was a pudgy little girl with black curly ringlets and such a quiet calm temperament for a four year old. Her constant companion was her little rag doll. Mama kept her for a few hours sometimes in the afternoon while her mother did her "Days Work." Back then "Days Work" meant cleaning and cooking for a white family up on the concourse. I enjoyed little Valerie immensely and looked forwarded to playing with her on the days her Mother left her with us. One day Sis. Beaman said she had to move back home with her family because she was not well and could not work anymore. The next week I watched a moving van across the street, pack their meager belongings, and drive away with little Valerie waving through the side window on her mother's lap. Tears of sorrow welled up in my eyes. This was a new emotion foreign to me. I did not know that saying "goodbye" could be so sad. I turned away and choked back a lump in my throat. Jeanie seemed braver than I or else she didn't mind or care that perhaps we would never see little Valerie or ever play with her again. I said to Jeanie as she sprang off the steps in front of the Tailor Shop. "If I ever have a little girl of my own I'm going to name her Valerie." Jeanie looked back at me in amazement and said, "how you gonna do that?" "You gotta get old like Mama first, and be just as smart." I said, I don't know how, but I'm gonna try real hard.

Muriel Ratteray Green

CHAPTER TWO

The Man of the Hour

When and how do you begin a story? Usually when your first recollections are screened on your mind. But then sometimes our memories tease, fail us, jump back and the least recent happenings seem to be the most important at the present time. I am who I am right now, doing saying, believing and acting out because of all the ingredients that went into my unconscious being; all the colored threads, dark hues, bright golden, shadowy purple, sewn into the pattern of my life make me what I am today.

I was a child born during the depression days. My early childhood was uneventful as far as personal trauma is concerned. My parents loved their little Mimsie and Jeanie and showed it by their constant care for us. I will never forget those early depression days. I remember the election of President Roosevelt to the Whitehouse little tike that I was. I remember sitting cross-legged with Jeanie on the old worn out Indian rug listening to his speeches on the radio. His voice was resonant and with clarity of speech he promised the American people a better time. He promised the "New Deal" which was an extensive Governmental program. Just how it operated or how it was implemented at that time I am not sure and neither have I searched it out for I am not a historian, but a humble teller of tales. But I do know that Mr. Roosevelt was the man of the hour and he did try and was successful in changing the course of his countrymen in his lifetime. During the time of the nineteen thirties' to the 1940's, people were poverty stricken. The economy was at its lowest ebb. Some hopeless folks had lost their life's savings during the Stock Market crash of 1929. Some resorted to alcohol and Skid Row, some turned suicidal and some turned to God. My parents had an abiding faith in the Lord Jesus Christ to carry them through adversity. Certainly with their hard work, self-denials and their implicit faith in God, they made it through those dismal dark days.

Getting up early on a Sunday morning and getting ready for Church was a part of the weekend ritual. Mama usually cooked on Saturday for Sunday's dinner. Clothes were "laid out" on Saturday evening for Sunday morning service. Daddy buffed and shined everyone's shoes and lined them in the windowsill neatly in size places. And oh! My! How I do remember Sunday morning service! How could any one child forget those earliest experiences? We attended a mission church about three blocks away from our apartment. I must have been very young at the time because I cannot recall my exact age, but I do remember a lady named Sis Curtis. A very tall white lady with blond flowing hair, dressed in white from neck to ankles and with a wide silver belt sash around her waist. A tambourine in her hand and a voice like a songbird she sang loud and clear. "Come to Jesus, Come to Jesus, Come to Jesus, just now, He will save you, He will save you, He will save you just now."

I don't remember when or where I did come to Jesus, but I do know that I had to go to Him. I do know that I could not have made it in this life if I did not go to Him, and after coming to Jesus, He did receive me as a little child.

Then there was the big Red Brick Church, that they called "Mother Horns" Tabernacle somewhere in the heart of Harlem. We visited their a number of times, riding on the Lexington Ave train, getting off at 125th Street, walking west in the heart of Harlem until we came to this great red brick building with the cross on the outside. The red and blue letters were very impressive across the front doors. Mama read the words out loud every time we came. "Revival Time with Mother Horn. Come and Be Blessed."

Inside the ladies were dressed in their Sunday best. Everything smelled good and fresh. Everyone was tiptoeing about, shaking hands with each other and everyone was smiling. The young men at the great front doors wore white gloves. When they walked you to your seat, they held out one hand in front of them and the other one behind their backs. The chairs on the podium were covered in a deep plushy purple. The long oblong table in the front of the podium was covered with a beautiful white lacy covering, the likes of which I had never seen before. In the middle of the table was a tall crystal pitcher with two tall glasses on a tray. I strained my neck to see and hear everything. My patent leather shoes did not touch the floor, but Jeanie's long legs and feet were on the ground. Daddy's knees were crossed in front of him. Mama held tightly on to her tiny beaded purse. Everyone waited in anticipation. We waited and watched while the seats filled up and there arose a din of hushed voices around us.

Eventually a tall stringy man in a long black robe with as I thought his collar was on backwards began praying. He tilted his head all the way backwards and locked his hands over his head. I had never seen anyone pray this way before, and it fascinated me. He appeared to be pushing the high ceiling away from his head. I stood on tiptoe and looked around me. Mama & Daddy's eyes were closed, and their lips were moving. "Dear Father in heaven," he repeated over and over and over again. Hear us when we pray to thee." I could not hear everything the tall man was saying, because the people all around us seemed to be helping him to pray. When the prayer was finally over a lady stood up and started a song. The piano in the corner helped her find the right tune. "He brought me out of the Miry Clay" she sang. "He planted my feet on a rock to stay." "He put a song in my soul today, a song of praise Hallelujah!" Everyone was smiling and singing and nodding to each other. Daddy was tapping his feet with his knees going up and down to the beat of the music. I felt all tingly and happy inside. When the song was finished someone got up to testify. Another jumped up to testify. This lady was throwing her arms all about. I could not tell if she was crying or laughing. But she did not seem unhappy. She was praising her God. She kept shouting, "This is real, real, real. Her eyes were shut tight, her white teeth flashing. She brought out a powered hankie from the top of her dress and waved it all around, then they sang some more until she finally sat down in her seat.

Soon it was collection time. Two ladies dressed in white uniforms marched to the front of the audience and stood straight and tall each with a basket in her hands. Jeanie said to me, whispering in her cupped hand, "They are Nurses, and they'll put that thermometer in you if you're not a good girl. A shudder ran down my back I remembered having my temperature taken at the clinic in the beginning of the year when I had a sore throat. My mind became confused. Jeanie was up to no good again. Her greatest joy in life at that time was teasing me. Yes, she was tricky and always tried to give me a fright. I looked up at her black button eyes. She seemed confident and self composed as she twisted her long black braids. I sat back in my chair and began swinging my feet, I had my braids to comfort me also. "They are not Nurses," I said to myself. Nurses don't live inside churches; they live inside the clinics where they give the needles. They looked more like the Laundry Ladies I had seen marching in front of a big grey building, carrying signs and calling out "Give us back our jobs." But those ladies marching on the avenue in front of the big Grey building did not wear white gloves as these ladies did. These ladies wore a cross with a gold & purple ribbon on their left breasts. Daddy called these ladies "Ushers," whatever that meant. These ladies seemed to know their job thoroughly. They knew how to empty those crispy bills from one basket to the next. They grabbed young babies from their mothers when their cries interrupted the minister's loud pleadings. Their white swinging shirts swishing quickly, when fans were suddenly needed. I looked up at Jeanie and whispered quietly, "I'm gonna be a husher when I grow up, thinking that was their job to "Hush the babies" and quiet down all unnecessary confusion during those Sunday morning services.

Mama made arrangements for me to be baptized in the church pool and on a Palm Sunday morning. Mama first asked me, "Do you love Jesus?" I said, "Oh! yes I do. I suddenly felt that I did love Jesus. Mama said, "well if you do love Jesus, then He is your personal savior, and He dwells in your heart; and you should be baptized to let the world know that you are a Christian. One evening Daddy took out his big Bible and sat Jeanie and I down on the couch in the living room and read to us about a man named John, who was sent from God to teach people about the man Christ Jesus. That night before I went to sleep I pictured in my mind this man John The Baptist running down our Avenue carrying signs like the ones I had seen, and Mama read out loud "Give Mr. Roosevelt your vote." My mind was alert and vivid although a little child. Somehow I was able to grasp the simple meaning of a situation although maybe not the whole implication when first presented with that situation.

Now the word baptize was a new word to me. I pondered it over many days in my mind. Mama said a nice minister was going to dip me down so quickly in a pool of water. So quickly she emphasized that I would not have time to remember it. Jeanie did not seem interested in such a happening. She did not state that Jesus had come into her heart. So Mama and Daddy did not force her to be baptized and so she watched and listened to all the happenings from the sidelines. At times her eyes twinkled, and her voice giggled at me. Jeanie is the smart one I thought, this selfish girly sister of mine whom I loved so dearly, and I whom she only wanted to tease. She seemed at times to know the answers to all the secrets of the world, but kept them locked up behind her broad brown brow. Did she know what baptize meant? Why didn't Jeanie consent to be dipped in a water pool as I did? Had she let Jesus come into her heart? She was only a few years older than I. Why did she act as if she were one hundred years older. I knew that the words one hundred really meant forever, and if anyone lived to be that old that they knew everything there ever was to know. That particular Palm Sunday rolled around and a beautiful clear bell like day it was. I will never in this lifetime forget the day and the experience it brought me if I live to be one hundred.

Mama brought Jeanie and I to the big red brick church where "Mother Horn" was there in person. I do not remember Daddy being there. He might have been studying his books that day. It must have been "Children's Day" for there were lots of little girls and boys my age and older running all around. But I noticed smart brave Jeanne was now holding on to Mama's gloved hand, and was saying very little to me. Soon I and the other children that were to be baptized were taken to a back room that opened into a beautiful Hall with flowers and pictures painted on the walls. On one wall was a beautiful picture of the boy Jesus with his eyes wide open looking up to heaven, and his hands folded together. Over his head was the brightest blue white dove with outstretched wings. Over Jesus' head was a golden hazy glow, and I learned in later years that this was his glory. The children were now separated from their parents, and two ladies dressed in white, took care of us. They helped us into our long white robes, and kept us quiet in a circle. I could see behind a curtain, some purple velvet steps and a stage. The pool was in the stage and all the relatives and friends were in the audience waiting and watching.

I was not sure of just what was going to happen, or how or where. But, I was not afraid or disturbed, just in great anticipation. The audience outside the curtains sang many choruses; one of which was "Jesus Loves Me this I Know." A Minister got up to speak. Then another Minister got up to speak. I was beginning to get warm in my robe. The other children were becoming noisy and restless. I watched everything and everyone and began to wonder. Then the piano began to tinkle some beautiful notes. The curtain slid back on each side and we were beckoned onto the stage towards the two Ministers that stood side by side, and the beautiful pool of water with flower petals floating on top, and the sweetest perfumed aroma I had ever encountered. Mama said later on that evening that I smelled like honey suckle rose, and I knew with joy in my heart where the smell had come from.

Oh how happy I felt. I was completely exhilarated. I moved across the stage in my white stocking feet waiting my turn. My name was called, and I went forward to two pairs of waiting arms. They folded my arms across my chest and whispered quietly, "Hold your breath, dear little one." "In the name of The Father, The Son and The Holy Ghost we do baptize thee."

I do not remember going under, I do not remember coming up, it all happened so quickly. But I do remember Dancing, dancing, dancing all over the stage, in and out, up and down. They were playing, Yes Jesus loves me, Yes Jesus loves me, Yes Jesus loves me, for the Bible tells me so. Mama was behind me and in front of me trying to steady me so I would not bump myself or fall off the stage. She had a big towel in her hand that she held out to dry me with. When she finally reached me she hugged me and kissed me and loved me and held me tight to her bosom as I had never been held in my life. She smiled directly into my eyes and I saw the tears of joy well up into her eyes. "I know you are very happy "she said this is the joy that comes from knowing Jesus. Now I was beginning to understand. Something new, fresh and good was happening to me on the inside. She continued, "and as you grow older you will understand it more." "You will never ever forget this event. She dressed me quickly and wrapped me in a little pink angora sweater she had brought along for me. I don't want you to get a chill she said. I said to myself, being baptized is one of the best things that could ever happen to a little child such as I. I looked at Jeanie now hiding behind Mama's waistline. Her eyes had narrowed down and her mouth was not smiling. She was pouting, or put out, maybe neglected, for this was the first time in our girlhood that we did not share something together. I reached for her hand; she pulled it back and wiped it on her dress. Then throwing her braids over her shoulders she turned her back to me.

I noticed a change in Jeanie after the event of the Baptismal service. As I look back on it now, I realize that Jeanie was growing up and leaving her baby days where as I was still the baby in the family, and now Jeanie although still at a very tender young age was allowed the privilege of making choices for herself. Jeanie liked drawing with her crayons and colored pencils. She was drawing everything in sight. One day she copied a picture of Mae West from the newspaper with her curly blond hair and sultry red mouth. Mama and Daddy were delighted that she was showing such talent. She hung about Mama in the kitchen. She learned all the girly things that little girls learn in their pre-teen days. She helped to make corn muffins and watched wide-eyed as Mama plucked the chickens and soaked them in lemon juice for roasting in the big flat iron stove. I was much more interested in playing games and listening to the radio. I loved listening to the radio especially when Daddy had it turned down low to one of those fancy music stations as he called it. I know now that Daddy had a real taste for some of the finer things of life.

When Daddy switched on the radio, he would lean over with his two elbows on his knees and his ear cocked to the meshed microphone. Some boxing events would greatly excite him. "Some young fellow is gonna win the title" he called out to Mama. "That Brown Bomber's got lead in his punch." Then one day the News Broadcaster burst forth with an ominous story. That great big beautiful balloon,

The Hindenburg, cruising in the sky over New Jersey had burst into flames. The next day the newspapers were full of the bold black print. Daddy brought home a newspaper every evening with a big 2 cent sign in each corner. All the news fit to print for 2 cents. I looked at the picture in the centerfold. The ladies wore tight flat hats to their heads. They peeked out of one eye, while the other eye was covered with a crimped wave of hair. Shoes were pointed at the toes and ladies heels looked like spools of thread. All the men wore grey covers over their shoes that they called spats and walked with a walking stick. People were dancing something called a Lindy Hop or the Big Apple, or maybe the both together. They were truckin' on down the Avenue, with not a single thing to do."

There was a King over in Great Britain name Edward. He loved an American Divorced woman so well that he walked away from his throne in order to marry her. I kept everything in the back of my mind. Nothing passed me by, little girl that I was in a changing world. Yes the world was changing, and does ever change. Nothing remains the same. The only reality of it is that during the world's progress, whether for the good or bad of it, we all become a part of it. We take part in the changes, help to carve out its history, and put together the pieces of this great puzzle of life. Jeanie was changing. Mama and Daddy were changing. The world was changing. I was living in a very impressionable time in my life and was not aware of it then. They were called the Pre-War days of WW II.

Daddy decided to take a job with the W.P.A. This was the Worker Progress Administration, a program that employed over a million people and probably helped to jumpstart the economy during that period in this country. I do remember the bread lines and the soup kitchen. But we were never made to feel poor. Mama knew how to make the tastiest bread puddings made with penny rolls from the bakery enhanced with raisins and grated cinnamon sticks. We had a huge flattop black iron stove, which took small shovels of black coal. Here she did all her cooking.

I also remember the NRA; a red white and blue sticker with an Eagle in the middle was another one of Mr. Roosevelt's programs. The NRA stood for the National Recovery Administration. This program might not have been quite successful because it was soon abandoned. There were other relief programs, and the "New Deal' was the catch word of the times. While the U.S.A. struggled to stir up economical growth within our country, there was growing a gloomy cloud over the European Horizon. Someone by the name of Hitler was stirring up tensions among the European countries. These tensions spilled over into the Daily Newspapers and magazines. This man's picture with the broom brush mustache and beady eyes adorned the front pages of the newspapers and magazines. Shockwaves and ripples of fear and insecurity were reaching our shores. It seemed as though those depression days were slowly fading in the wake of certain awareness. The U.S. had to prepare and protect them from outside aggression. The plowshares and pruning hooks had failed us during the depression, and were now being exchanged for tanks and guns. Ironically these massive undertakings during the last half of the 1930's brought a wind-down to the depression and stimulated the economy with Mr. Roosevelt at the helm of his great Ship of State.

CHAPTER THREE

Intermediate Days

Holidays had special meanings for Jeanie and me. I don't remember Christmas showing up on the calendar as early as it does these days. In fact right after Halloween, we had to eat the Thanksgiving Turkey first, digest it, throw out the wrack and let the digestive juices calm down before tackling the Christmas dinner and all its trimmings.

The Christmas celebration was primarily a religious experience in our home. Santa Clause and his reindeers coming down the chimney, we understood at an early age was only a myth. Christmas tree, glitter and toys were O.K. but it never took the place of the real meaning of Christmas. Christmas meant the birth of the Christ child. Jesus the Savior of the world. The church we attended put on their exercises during the Christmas week. Carols, skits, poems, pantomime all depicting the poignant story of the first advent of Christ to this planet Earth. Jeanie and I always took part in these exercises. We went to practice on Wednesday afternoon after school to the community church on Prospect Ave. Upstairs in the great hall were seats for about 200 people. Sister Ellison, the minister's wife always at the piano held sway. She taught about thirty pre-teens and teens, to sing, recite and to love God and one another.

The Full Gospel Community Church on Prospect Ave was around the corner from the candy store and Daddy's Tailor Shop. The Tailor shop had to be closed as I mentioned before because of the shortage of oils and other important commodities during WW II.

Easter Sunday was another Holiday that is unforgettable and holds precious memories. Our church was decorated with Easter Lilies and pink and white carnations usually hand made by the most talented First Lady of our church, Sister Ellison. She taught us our songs and anthems heralding the Risen Christ. Up from the Grave He arose, with a Mighty Triumph Ore His Foes. We did not know then, how blessed and privileged we were to have someone so interested in us. "The Community Young People, as we were called. The girls usually wore white blouses and black shirts. No sneakers or bobby socks were allowed, not when we were scheduled to sing before the congregation. The young fellow's dressed in their dark suits and white shirts and navy ties. We strung across the platform and in front of the piano. Our church did not have an organ during those early days, but I am sure that the music we made was beautiful and truly blessed the heart of God. We sang the early Gospel songs and the old Time Spirituals and the audience loved us. There was always cookies and hot chocolate served afterwards in the little kitchen by some of the mothers of the church. These were good Old Fashioned happy days for us even though a war was being fought on distant lands. We thanked God that no bombs had fallen thus far on the mainland of the USA. We had our friends and buddies. We paired off in our little groups and clicks as all society does. But we had one underlying watch ward that was Love. Love and understanding for each other. I know now, that was what the minister and his good wife were trying to teach their Young People.

Sometimes there were differences and misunderstandings but there was always a way to solve these misunderstandings. The way was Jesus and at the altar. After church service was the altar where anyone could come and kneel and pray. The lights would be turned down low. Soft hymns would be hummed by a few around the piano. Hands clapped and arms stretched upward towards heaven, they would call out to Jesus, to bless, forgive and renew. These were the intermediate days for all of us. We were young innocent and so vulnerable. The world was in chaos and moving towards a very shattering experience of which we were oblivious. "Take Jesus into your heart, take Him with you everywhere you go." We believed and many of us committed ourselves to the Lord Jesus Christ, to be the Lord in our lives. If we had not done so, I do believe that the survival rate of those Young People, through that transitional period would have been very small.

One quiet Sunday afternoon on December 7th 1941 was a day of "Infamy" as our President Roosevelt called it. The Japanese attacked Pearl Harbor. The U.S. was not ready for such a military attack. We were instantly thrown into war. There was no deliberation. The Army, Navy and The Marines reported to their stations immediately. I can remember the incident clearly as if it happened yesterday. We were living in the Bronx apartment at the time. Mama and Daddy had the Sunday pages between them. We had been to church earlier in the morning and we were just sitting around after our Sunday dinner. Jeanie was busy with her schoolwork on the end of the Dining table, and I was at the piano. I loved the piano and could play sufficiently enough to amuse myself. I had been taking lessons from a very unrelenting rules tapping lady named Madam Bonner. For one dollar an hour she would put me through a very grueling time period, determined to make a pianist of me. But for some reason I relented and did not return to her after a half dozen lessons. But I loved the piano and did not fail to go to the keys every day to play the hymns of the church. So I was at the piano on this particular Sunday afternoon in our living room that was next to our Apartment door.

Suddenly I heard doors in the outside vestibule opening and closing. Hushed voices talking excitedly. I stopped playing and hurried to the door to listen. Mrs. Seabrook from across the hall was saying. "Put on your radio, you'll hear it now." Her voice was quick and high pitched. "Yes it true," she repeated again, "Its true," "We're in war," "We're in war." Old Captain was standing in his doorway with cane in hand, tapping and sputtering in disbelief. "Well I'll be a Monkey's Uncle," he said over and over again as he turned back inside his apartment door. I ran back to Daddy and Mama in their room. "Mrs. Seabrook says we're in war, she heard it on the radio." Daddy took three leaps from his chair by the window, papers flying everywhere. "My God," he exclaimed, I knew it would be sooner than later. He switched on the Emerson radio and played with the knobs until we heard the worried voice of Gabriel Heather.

Yes, Pearl Harbor had been bombed on Dec 7, 1941 and we received the news on a quiet Sunday afternoon. This attack crippled and surprised the U.S. Naval fleet and destroyed its strategic basis. The U.S. was surprised and unprepared for such an onslaught of fighting. Now we were officially at war with Japan. Great Britain became our Ally. Whether that high stepping, arm saluting Hitler in Germany was prepared to fight the allies or not, I do not know, but the whole world was in turmoil and this was becoming a Global War. This was the Second World War fought in the country that started in 1941 and lasted until 1945. The U.S. was smiled upon during these dark days. The fighting on land and sea & the Air Strikes never took place on our shores. Yet its intensity, scope, and scale are unparalleled in the annals of History. The actual detonation of nuclear weapons, catapulted the world into the Atomic Age.

I was thirteen years old at the start of World War II. Jeanie was fifteen years.

Mama suddenly became very patriotic. The big vegetable market on Prospect Ave in the Bronx closed down its sheds and the Red Cross moved in. Long metal folding tables and chairs to match were soon lined up on the hard concrete floors of the old market place. Large boxes of rolled gauze-like material arrived in white paper wrappings marked "Official, Red Cross." A big white flag with the Red Cross in the center hung over the center of the double door entrance. The American flag hung along side of the Red Cross Flag. This gauze had to be cut and rolled into bandages for our wounded men. Mama and Jeanie enrolled with Red Cross people to denote a certain amount of hours every week to roll bandages. Summer days after the Declaration of war found Jeanie at the Red Cross Center. I went along with Mama and Jeanie to watch or help the Ladies count and box the bandages. After they were cut, folded, counted and boxed they had to go to another location where they were sterilized before being sent to the fighting men overseas.

Jeanie had a new aura about her now. She no longer wore two long braids. She was fifteen. She wore her hair in a pompadour and a pageboy, which hung around her shoulders like a tent. I was allowed to comb my own hair now, but I did not know how to style it. There was so much of it. I watched Jeanie as she combed, brushed greased and subdued her hair into the style she was pleased with. On a few occasions she tried to help me try out some new hairstyles. But her hands felt too heavy on my head, and she protested that I was too "tender headed" to endure her rakings through my scalp because that's what it felt like to me. I was so used to Mamas gentle touch on my head that even after those vigorous scrubbings and brushings I did not flinch from her hands. I often wondered later on was Jeanie's hands that rough on the other ladies that she worked on.

Jeanie was growing into a beautiful young lady. A girl in her teens in the thirty's and forties was not considered a woman at fifteen. But if she was sweet, kind, obedient and respectful to her elders she was considered a young lady. It seemed to everyone that Jeanie fit the bill. Everyone called her young Lady, and I noticed an unusual glow about her. Her skin was a creamy beige and her eyebrows, which used to be thick and bushy, seemed to be thinning and arching at the corners most likely with the help of a pencil liner that Mama kept on her dresser with her small fingernail scissors. Her breasts had rounded and her long legs had stopped skipping after me. She began moving her hips and shoulders when walking. She had a few new girlfriends who she whispered with after school. She seemed to be gaining more freedom from Mama's watchful eyes, yet Mama was always around watching and questioning. We came home from school now at different times, but Mama was always there when we got home. Mama and Daddy allowed us to travel back and forth from school without Mama. They had quiet little talks together in the kitchen. Jeanie always liked to help Mama cook. Now she was really making the whole dinners, when Mama allowed it.

She could fry chicken until it was crispy and golden. She knew how to make beef stew from scratch; not like the kind you got out the can, browning the flowered beef chunks in hot oil just the way Mama taught her. Jeanie could straighten up the kitchen in a shake of a lambs tail so said Mama after she pulled out all the pots and pans. Daddy was also proud of his oldest daughter Jeanie. Yes she was becoming a prize. Not only could she cook and clean, she could sew and draw anything she laid her eyes on.

Jeanie discovered the hot straightening comb, and this made her popular with the sisters in the church. They would wash their hair early Saturday mornings and Jeanie would have them hot combed out, with the help of Dixie Peach pomade in a matter of an hour's time. She also knew how to make brown bag paper curlers for styling. This way she was able to make pocket money. Jeanie once won a "Draw Me" contest from the Daily Newspapers. A representative of the contest came to our home and wanted to enroll Jeanie in art classes. Mama and Daddy looked at each other. This was a new undertaking, where would they get the money for her books and supplies. But Jeanie surprised us all. " I don't want to go to Art School, I already know how to draw." And indeed she did know how to sketch or copy anything she saw in the newspaper or magazines. "I really want to sew, she continued." "I want to design clothes." "I want to make hats and dresses and anything that makes a lady look pretty. This was something new, Mama and Daddy had to ponder over. Jeanie had real fresh talent and should have special training.

Charles and Joanna Ratteray did not worry and agonize over the future. I'm not certain whether they should have or not. They did not worry about the rationing of oil for cars and machines. The rationing of food or the use of the food tokens. Some people were hoarding. Sugar, Crisco and meat were becoming bargaining agents. The Black Market came into being. What you could not buy legitimately of short supply you could get under the table for a price. But Mama and Daddy lived by the Golden Rule and prayed for the peace of the World. Everyone wore Red Cross buttons. The American flag appeared in windows of homes and shops. Daddy put up dark green shades at the windows to be pulled down during the "Black Outs." The sirens would wail at any given time day or night, mimicking a surprise attack. Everyone had to take shelter inside or off the streets. All lights turned out and shades pulled down if the Air Raid exercise was nighttime. My Uncle Robert become an Air Raid Warden in Brooklyn. He wore an olive drab 2 piece uniform and Gas Mask during the practice. The people in the U.S. had great faith in God and their country. Somehow we weathered the storm, which was really only an inconvenience compared to the atrocities that occurred in the European Countries.

Maybe they should have planned further on in the future for both of their little girls. But who really could make concrete plans at all during those war years. They quietly accepted the days as they came and went, loving us and teaching us by example. They had no money reserves. Very few people did in those dismal days. Mama never worked outside the home after marrying Daddy, but we always had a home, love and the four of us were never separated. When Jeanie was growing into lady hood I was becoming very observant. Nothing missed my ears or eyes. Frankie Sinatra was the new big singing voice for the teen girls. Jeanie had a pair of brown and white shoes and white bobby socks. She knew all his songs and sang the words by heart. Sonja Henie had shot her way to fame. Everyday was a new happening. I took out my long thick braids and experimented with different hairstyles. These were my awakening days. I understood something new and different was to happen in my body. Mama had explained it all to me. I did not wince or shrink back but waited with anticipation.

CHAPTER FOUR

The Discovery

How do we discover ourselves? How does it come about? Do we wake up one morning look in the mirror and it all unfolds before our eyes. How does it come about that we suddenly realize who we are and the very reason for our existence? That we see ourselves separate and apart from everyone else, and with our own unique identity. This realization came to me early in life. I knew I belonged to and was part of a family. We had the same last name, bore likeness to and resembled family members in numerous inherited ways. But I knew early on that I was me, and that no one else in this world could duplicate me. But this was my guarded secret. A secret I had to keep to myself for the time being for fear I would be misunderstood. For fear others would label me as uppity or selfish and maybe both. I was not a lonely girl because I enjoyed my own company and became acutely aware of everything around me. I became in tune with my environment and my inner self at a very early age.

I loved Mama and Daddy immensely, and I think now as I look back that I loved Jeanie much more than she loved herself. Jeanie liked her many girlfriends. She liked clothes, clothes, and anything that had glitter and glamour. As a growing up girl she tried to copy everything that came along whether, style, dance or whatever was in vogue, and she did it with such flair and ingenuity that folks thought she had been to some Cosmopolitan Fashion School. She was certainly talented. She could sketch her ideas, sew and style different outfits from pieces of materials that Daddy left around from his Tailoring orders. She made hats and bags and sold them to whoever would buy from her. She could copy anyone of the latest hairstyles. She could cook anything and bake cakes and make fresh cookies, thanks to Mama's close tutoring. Mama said, "She'll make someone a good wife." Daddy answered hardly moving his lips, "When the times comes, he'll have to pass under my nose." Daddy was a man of a few words but when he answered something swiftly and with one sentence it had a profound meaning.

Jeanie was in her teen years and was looking towards the future; she was hoping that when the war ended, she would be able to enter into dress making business school. In fact this was always her girlhood dream. The one thing that Jeanie was not capable of doing was carrying a tune. Oh yes she would mouth the words and make a noise along with the rest of us, but sing, Jeanie could not. But even this, Jeanie capitalized on, yes on this one fact she could make everyone laugh. Everyone would go into hysterics when she sang off key. I will never forget the occasion when she and I were called upon to render a selection in song at our church. "Great is Thy Faithfulness." Everyone sat in rapt attention waiting for her voice to go off key and it did to everyone's amusement. So Jeanie's inability to carry a tune became a plus for her.

Jeanie and I suddenly became pals again in my early teens. I still enjoyed my quiet moments alone to myself, and she noticed and did not intrude. I loved to read, read, and read. If something was interesting I could not put it down until it was finished. I went to the library and spent hours among the autobiographies. I encouraged Jeanie to come with me, and she did on many occasions only to sit at the tables thumbing through the latest fashion magazines. Jeanie now became interested in me, and I was almost as tall as she although not as curvaceous or willowy. She once remarked to me as I was viewing myself in Mama's floor length mirror. "Its all there Mimsie, everything you need to be a beautiful woman it's all just got to wake up." I Looked at her nonplussed this was one of her rare serious moments with me and I suddenly felt rejuvenated, not that I wanted to be complemented, but I only wanted us to be friends. She helped me fix my hair and gave me a few of her dresses she thought was becoming. Mama was becoming a beaming matronly woman. She had two beautiful teen-age daughters as everyone said. I did not think myself beautiful. I knew that I was not, but I also knew that I could be a little more attractive if I allowed myself a wee bit. But somehow I was not interested in all that glamour. I was interested in drawing, reading, and more reading. I loved books and books were my friends. Daddy had volumes of books and maps and magazines. He had instructional books on how to repair cars, how to navigate boats and how to fly aircraft. One day when I was at his shelf taking out his books, for he never prohibited me from going through his books; only that I replaced them carefully he said to me; "I am a man with a lot of "How to", but I have not the "right to." I looked up as he was spreading out his cloth on his cutting table his jaws set tight, "What do you mean by that?" I queried. He turned about to me and rubbed his chin. "Mimsie" he said, after you "know how" you must be able "to show how." Daddy was a man of a few words, but this explanation was not sufficient for me. I pursued the matter. Tell me what you really mean I insisted. He made a deep sigh, which seemed to come from way down deep inside of him. "Girlie" he said which was a word he seldom used for either of us only on very few special occasions. "After you have studied on any single subject in this life whether spiritual or natural, you must pass tests set up by God or man. For there are standards of performance in everything." "Just reading on a certain subject does not make you proficient in that subject, you must have hands on experience in everything you study on." I understood now, when he returned back to his cutting board. Daddy had not had the opportunity to be and do all the things he read about in his books.

The Saturday Evening Post was Mama's favorite, along with the Look Magazine. I was never interested in household duties as I realize now that I should have been. I did not learn how to cook and Mama did not force it on me. Mama said, "She'll learn when the time comes for her, she'll learn." In my immense desire to read, I passed up nothing in print. I discovered the Bible. Not just the Bible Verses, the Psalms and stories we had to read for Sunday School, but that this book was like none other in all the world. Written over such a long span of time and by so many different authors yet it's sixty-six books was cohesive and spoke the same message. That the Messiah was promised, that he came to earth, was accepted by a few, finished the work here on this earth that his Father had given him to do, returned back to heaven to prepare a dwelling place for all those who believe on him and diligently follow his teachings. I thought on these things often, and now all the religious training that I had received in my home and in Church was beginning to connect.

I attended Eagle Jr. High School in the Bronx. At the top of the 163rd St. Hill on Eagle Ave. This was an All Girl's School attended by a good sprinkling of Italian, Irish, and about an even amount of colored girls as we were so called then. Nothing eventful transpired for me during that time except for my initiation into womanhood that I looked for but did not long for because at times I wanted to remain a little girl. But my inner self understood that I could not stay a curled tight little rosebud forever. The real me was waiting to burst forth and bloom into a real person. I was happy with myself contented to be alone with me. I could sing, and oh how I did sing! I joined the Glee club in Eagle Jr. High School. I loved poetry and even tried writing some small verses of my own. Mama was delighted with this and encouraged me greatly. She also was a bookworm. She often listened to me as I recited poems, while she prepared the supper, wiping her eyes on the end of her apron. Sis Ellison noticed me at church and gave me poems to read at some of her exercises. I was delighted and she allowed me to read some of my writings when she put on her church programs. Jeanie was now going to Jane Adams High School in the Bronx. A Trade School for girls where she took up the trade of dressmaking. Daddy thought this was just wonderful she was following in his footsteps. She was learning to be a seamstress. She learned to cut out patterns, making her own and draping. They also had a beauty Culture course at this school. She was learning two trades at the same time. Dress Making and Beauty Culture. She seemed very happy in her work and Mama and Daddy were pleased.

Now Jeanie and I had become bosom buddies. She always had some secret to tell me about her girlfriends for she had many at school, or about some of the young fellows at our church. She was vivacious and well liked and the fellows always buzzed around her. I never seemed to be noticed by the opposite sex. I think that I became a hindrance to Jeanie at this time because she was expected to always look out for me. Mama insisted, "Don't leave her out, and don't leave her behind." Mama always insisted that we go together, stay together and come home together whenever we attended these church programs. Ironically speaking it was at one of these church socials that Jeanie met her first and only love, Ronald. And was at one of these church picnics that I met Sam who was to become my life long friend and husband. But here I must stop myself for I do not want to get ahead of my story, because too much transpired before these events took place in our lives.

Well now during my teen years I was busy becoming Muriel. Mama and Daddy would always call me Mimsie. Aunt Bertie and Uncle Robert in Brooklyn called me Mula, which I hated with a passion. Mama was now calling me Muriel Darlin'. I knew who I was, I was that quiet calm little person, reaching out to be noticed and accepted by my family and peers. I understood that I had a soul, an inner spirit connected to God. I had given myself to God at an earlier age. I had allowed Jesus to come into my life. Whether it was by the association of the Church family or a personal experience to his teachings I was not sure at the time; but I do know that Jesus and His teachings had made a difference and a great impact in my life. He had come into my heart when I was a little girl. He was my everyday friend. He was with me day and night. I learned to call on him when I needed him and he was always there for me. He was my Savior and I trusted Him for the salvation of my soul. I read the Bible continuously and sang the hymns and Gospel songs over and over. There was always a deep stirring in my inner self when I was in church. I enjoyed my church services immensely. I loved to hear my Minister Rev. Ellison preach the word of God. I listened intently and then went home and opened my bible to compare his teachings with the bible. This was a beautiful time in my life. These were my days of discovering. Because I had suddenly discovered that God was real and in the Person of Jesus Christ, he was dwelling in the inner recesses of my soul. Oh what a delicious revelation! How could I keep this to myself? How could anyone else with the same experience keep it to himself or herself?

"What a Friend we have in Jesus" became my song of praise; I sang it, played it on the piano and hummed it every waking hour. "All our sins and grief's to bare, I knew for a surety that he had born all my sins on Calvary's Cross. Oh! the joy of it. Oh! the glory of it. I played the piano on occasion in Sunday school when Sis Frank could not make it to church and there was no one else to take her place. Sis Frank was my Godmother and Mama's best friend. At one time I had a little Sunday school class of seven little boys cute fidgety little fellows from four years to seven thereabouts. I taught them Bible verses and little rhyming songs. "His Banner Over Me is Love." was one of them. But "The Lords Army" was their favorite. They did not want to "Fly over the Enemy," "Shoot in the Artillery"," "Ride in the Calvary," they just wanted to be; "In the Lords Army."

These were beautiful days in my life. The in between years. Besides the new and abiding faith in God that I had recently discovered was the Muriel within me, and she was my very own best friend. Oh yes Jeanie was my pal we went places together and talked together about our other friends and shared jokes together. Anita who lived in the same block was one of my school chums. Soon another girl around my age came into our little circle of friends. She soon attached herself to me and I watching her and listening to her tales of woe began to take up with her and for her. Her name was Mary Fabian, and I will have to report that Mary's story was really a sad one. But the saddest part about her was that she really didn't know how unhappy drab and sorrowful her life really was. Everyone in school laughed at her because she was overweight and over developed in the wrong places. She had broken front teeth. As a young child she had suffered the ravages of rickets, which left her long leg bones badly deformed and loosened her front teeth. But I liked Mary Fabian for herself. She was not a clinging vine and pretended to herself and to all those around her that everything in her world was a'okay; I befriended her and we became buddies. But one day that friendship came to an end. I will speak no further on it right now as it would serve no purpose here and would be out of place in my story.

Jeanie and I had a special way communicating. Everyone we knew or almost everyone had a nickname. "Spin top" lived in the apartment house across the street from us. He was a teenage lad and was never without his spinning top when he bounced down the street to the corner candy store. Limp Foot lived around the corner on Union Avenue. He seemed well and happy but always dragged his left foot behind him. Sis Moochie Minnie, so named because she so reluctantly paid for her "hair dos" that Jeanie gave her every other week. Moochie Minnie would always say, "I'll pay you next week when my check comes in. We meant no harm, and had no animosity in our hearts to anyone. We made up songs and jingles about folks and laughed at our own jokes. These were special memorable days for me and I believe Jeanie thought the same also. Although we both had our own special friends we never forgot to be sisters. We borrowed each other junk and jewelry as we called it. Jeanie sewed up stuff for me, and I read and answered her mail to a soldier boy name Ronald who was stationed in Guam at the close of World War II when Jeanie was in her late teens.

The war had taken many of our young men away from the church circle. We gave them "going away" parties. We sang to them "God Will Take Care of You." "Through Everyday, O all the Way." He will Take care of You, (The you being held out for as long as you could hold your breath) "God Will Take Care of You." Then the young man who was leaving would sing back to the audience while his Mama in the audience wiped her eyes. "I'd Rather Have Jesus Than Anything;" or "Take the Name of Jesus With You." Almost everyone we knew now was in uniform. Either going away to wrap it up over there or returning home from war. If you did not know a soldier or sailor to write to, you became someone's Pen Pal. Everyone was writing or receiving letters from the Boys overseas written on paper-thin Air Mail paper. Exchanging pictures that was the thing to do that was patriotic. Keeping the morale up of the boys was very important. Jeanie's' Ronald was over there. She lived, walked, and talked Ronald from daylight to sunset. She had a little part time job on occasions with the Simplicity Pattern Company. She would work a few weeks at a time during summer months when she wasn't rolling bandages. Here she folded the patterns and slipped them into envelopes and was promised an opportunity to learn more about the job. Whether that was an empty promise or a surety who could tell? Jeanie was a colored girl, and there were white girls working along side of her but I am sure not half as talented as Jeanie. Here a new word bigotry, raised it ugly head. We were beginning to learn that the colored folks did not get a fair share, were not treated equally as others, and that their assets, talents and capabilities were not fairly considered when it came to jobs, housing etc. The war brought this to my attention. My inexperienced sheltered mind was opening up to the world around me. The colored soldiers fought for their country on foreign soil but were second-class citizens upon returning home.

Now they were calling the colored people Negroes. Negro is another word for black, which is all right if you are referring to the Black Race. But when you use the word Negro in a derogative way and shorten it; to nigger than it is an evil slanderous word. Now I often heard this word bandied about. "Negro," sometimes being misused as nigger under the guise of a slip of the tongue or a southern accent. Then it was used to describe some of the poor unfortunate children of the Southlands. Their pictures were being portrayed in bold magazine prints, standing by their family shacks, their scrawny arms hugging their Mama's swollen bodies big with child. These pockets of poverty in the South were called Nigger Towns. Here white wooly haired Grandpa's puffing on their corncob pipe came to the forefront of prize winning photography contests. Their sad plight helped the sale and circulation of these newspapers and magazines. Oh! How could this be? But yes it was and still is so. The Negro race was and to a degree now in this day and age is the most cast off and forgotten race of people, and right here in the Good old USA. I am using the word Negro now, because that is the term used then in the 1940's. This is only part of the Discovery for me. A hurtful part, a festering wound. A sick bandaged up part of a race of people supposedly created equal with the same rights as others. They were abused and used as their forefathers were, and when the job was done, whatever the job was, be it wars, railroads, cotton fields, they were thrown back on the trash heap of humanity, with little opportunity for enlightenment or survival. The Negroes had to scramble and scratch their way out of the bind that they were in. This was new information for me. I was a teenager, but my eyes were opening up too and my brain was becoming fine tuned to the environment around me and the current situation in the world. I tried to question Mama and Daddy about these new discoveries of mine. Mama said she didn't have any concrete answered for me. Daddy said, "I'm glad you're wide awake girlie." I had been living in a sheltered world, but I knew now, I had to shake myself, spread my wings and prepare myself for the outside world.

Yes the U.S. did have some inconvenience during the war days, because of the rationing of the foodstuffs, goods and supplies. The manufacturing of and production of Home Appliances had to be curtailed because every ounce of manpower was needed to fight in the war. But the U.S. did not suffer the ravages and bloodshed of war as some of our allies. God was with us and granted us the Victory over the enemy. But there was an internal enemy plaguing our country as I mentioned before. It was soon to shoot up its ugly head now and then, to be hurriedly pushed down forcefully in place like a jack-in-the-box. The name of this hideous enemy was discrimination. It existed all along hiding, undetected, sometimes being swept under a rug of disguise such as inadequacy.

Yes the Muriel inside of that young teenage girl was making new discoveries. Good ones and bad ones. I was also learning what the lessons of life had to offer. Life is not a bed of roses. Not April showers followed by May flowers. There was bitterness, hatred and contempt all around. There was sickness, distresses and disappointments. There was abusiveness, pain, suffering and mental anguish, and if you lived long enough in this world, some of these traumas would touch your life.

I became very reflective. I listened to my English teacher, Mrs. Ramsay. I went to the Library. I listened intently to the news stories on the radio. I read my bible. The Bible became my best friend. The Rev. Ellison said the Bible was the roadmap for the journey from Earth to Heaven. Knowing is better than not knowing. I felt I had an edge on everyone I was learning all about myself, who I was, how I got here and my purpose for being. I found that there was a disruptive force in the universe, and I also understood that there was a calm quiet gentle spirit surrounding those who sought after it. This spirit and still is the Spirit of God in the person of Jesus Christ.

Oh! what a discovery I had made, to realize that there was another strong reliable being, that could be depended upon to always be there for you in your hour of need, and to realize that this person was always there even before you knew yourself, for He Himself chose you to be his follower. What an eye-opener! What a mind boggler! That God the Father, Maker of the Universe, came down to man in the person of Jesus Christ, made provisions for my salvation, by dying on the cross for me; arose from the grave, is now in heaven preparing a place for me in the heavenlies when life's toil is ended. These facts humbled me and at the same time gave me a peaceful spirit.

I enjoyed being alone with my Bible, and myself so I could read the beautiful words of God and never was I lonely. I would sing, pray and meditate on whatever I had recently learned. Muriel, myself and I were best friends. We were in partnership with God. God was King over the entire Universe, the ruling force in the world and had the last say in His Kingdom of Righteousness and I was a child of The King.

CHAPTER FIVE

In The Interim

My high school days were a very critical period at this time of my life. I attended Morris High School in the Bronx. A beautiful old Gothic building on Boston Road and 167th Street with a spacious campus. This was an exciting time of my life. It was the door closing on my girlhood and one opening up to new beginnings. I opened the door stealthily and with trepidation, peeping slowly as I entered. Mama and Daddy did not hold me down to any given rules and regulations. They simply stated their expectations for their two daughters. The did not preach at us constantly, but setting the example, they held faith with God. I know now that Mama must have spent quiet a few hours in her prayer closet, talking to the Lord about her daughters. How else could we have survived the jumbled up world that was waiting for us in those post war days. I attended Morris High School in the mid 1940's. During that time, a lot had transpired, including the end of World War II on Sept 25th 1945. Coming from an all girls' Jr. High School to a Co-Ed Campus was pretty exciting to me.

Mama became very generous. She took me to Alexander's' Dept. Store on Third Ave in the Bronx for an unexpected shopping spree. She bought me "Little extras" as she called them. She did not want me to seem frivolous as she stated, but she knew I would have looked very dowdy and dull, if she did not take matters into her own hands. She bought me clips and combs for my hair, and dickey collars, pink, blue and white to be worn under my two sloppy Joe sweaters. The sweaters were oversized with shaggy fibers. Everyone wore the sleeves pushed up to the elbows. At this time everyone was wearing a plaid jacket of some sort. Mama bought me one. I marveled over these expenditures. She had saved and scrimped from her home babysitting jobs just for the event. It seemed Mama enjoyed these shopping joints more than I did.

Daddy was much more practical. He bought me a raincoat and a pair of boots. He traced my shoes on a piece of brown paper wrapping and came home from work one night with the boots and raincoat under his arm. Daddy always visited Canal Street in Manhattan where you could get anything different or odd at a cut-down price if you knew the art of haggling. Here he bought his bright colored spools of thread and materials for his Tailoring jobs. Here on Canal Street is where he saw this unusual green Khaki raincoat for a price, and here is where the boots were thrown in for a price. As I looked at the raincoat, I could not imagine myself wearing such a hideous garment. It appeared to me to be someone's left over army garb. I tried to make my face smile when I thanked him for both the raincoat and the boots. I did not want him to know how really disgruntled I was over them, and hoping it wouldn't rain for a good long time.

But the rain came soon, and I was very reluctant to wear this ugly green raincoat. It was such an odd dusty looking color. It had deep patch pockets and an attached hood. It had two top breast pockets, side slit pockets and another set of pockets with flaps under the waistline. It had an enormous long belt with a metal bronze buckle. The wide collar and lapels had the U.S. Army insignia on it. I was sure I did not want to be caught dead wearing the monstrosity of a raincoat and for the first time in my life I felt a strong sense of rebellion. I worried about what would the kids at school think of me sporting such a coat. I knew they would really laugh and probably crack jokes. Teenage kids have always been cruel to each other at some time in their lives and here and now I was looking to be accepted by my peers. It was natural and right to want to be accepted. These thoughts ran through my mind as I finally fell asleep that evening when Daddy brought the bundle home under his arm.

I woke up early the next morning and they're still in the dawn's shadow hung the raincoat on the outside of the closet door. I wondered to myself. Was Muriel changing? Was she becoming a different person? No, just another side of me was showing through. I was growing and emerging, trying out my wings, and at the same time I did not want to stand out like a sore thumb in any group or crowd. The real Muriel was still on board, comforting and keeping company with her own self-image. I recognized my likes and dislikes. I didn't like limelight and didn't want to be noticed too much and the raincoat certainly was an eye catcher. Two days after the coat arrived, it poured down buckets of rain. I had no other fit rainwear at the time. Mama said Daddy bought the raincoat just in time for his Mimsie. I was really exasperated now at this point, for Mama and Daddy still calling me Mimsie and for the coat staring back at me swinging limply from the back of our closet door. I had no other choice I had to don that hateful looking piece of apparel and I did so with indignation.

I was late that morning to school and as I hurried up the main entrance slushing wet, I heard the second bell ring. That was the late bell and meant all locker doors had to be closed and all corridors cleared of the students. I had just enough time to reach my home room class before the singing of "The Star Spangled Banner" by the Student body, for no one could move about during this exercise. I slipped in just in time and took my place in the second row at the second seat in my homeroom class. All eyes were on me or at least I thought so, for I was seldom late for classes. My mind was racing now. How could Daddy buy such a thing for me and expect me to wear it. Because of Lateness I was not able to hang my coat in my locker and had to carry it about with me until the third period class which was a free study period. I walked about from class to class with my wet raincoat until it dried itself off then hung it up in my locker during my study period. That coat made its mark on me that day and quite a few of inquisitive kids.

"Where did you get that?" They inquired. "I want one just like it," they stated. "Haven't you seen the latest?" they shouted at each other. "All the kids in the Village are wearing the Army leftovers!" I was nonplussed. I couldn't believe my ears. My ugly old green Army raincoat was a hit with the Morris-ites. They bombarded me with questions. Did you get it in a shop in the Village, or on Canal Street" I did not know where either place was. I only knew that Daddy saw a bargain and knew how to haggle the right price for something he wanted for his daughter. It seemed that old Army coats and jackets were becoming a fashion trend. Especially the oversized raincoats and Battle jackets. Here Daddy was one jump ahead of me and I was disappointed in my conduct and especially that I did not trust his judgment.

Basically I liked plain and simple things, not too frilly or fussy. I liked sweaters and shirts. I never wore socks in high school. I always wore stocking and brown penny loafers. I was glad to be free of the Auditorium blues, which were white middie blouses and blue navy skirts which we wore in Jr. High School. I could pick out and coordinate my own outfits from day to day and eventually my Army raincoat became my best friend. I actually enjoyed sporting it with its unusual wide lapels and deep patch pockets. I wore it every day except when the weather became too cold and blistery.

My days in Morris H.S. were learning days and fun days. Looking back now I realize that these were some of the best carefree days of my life. I joined different clubs and made new friends. Anita a good school chum lived in the corner house where Daddy had the Tailor shop. Mary Fabian became my best friend. We walked home from school everyday, and spent many hours after school talking about Jesus and Mama. Mary Fabian seemed starved for friendship. She was not a pretty girl. She was buxom with a beautiful singing voice. Oh! how Mary could sing. She sang the blues and all the love ballads and latest hits. But she was a very sad young lady as I learned later on. She was one of seven children. Jeanie and I visited her on occasion and sometimes we shopped together on Prospect Ave. Her family seemed to be always moving or in the process of moving. Boxes, unpacked barrels and crates stood about in every corner of their living room. Laundry was draped from lines strung over the sink in the kitchen. She seemed embarrassed at times but Jeanie and I pretended not to notice the disarray of her home. They lived in four huge rooms on the top floor of a narrow walk up tenement building on Prospect Ave. Her mother was a heavyset stern faced West Indian lady. She never wore shoes in the house but kept on a floppy wide brimmed hat, as if to shade her from the sun that was not shining in those dark dank rooms.

Fish and rice was their main dish. I don't remember smelling anything else cooking in that kitchen but fish. Her father worked in the open fish market on Fulton Street in downtown Manhattan. I loved Mary Fabian at the time, she was my dearest friend. I loved her and felt sorrow for her at the same time. I sorrowed at the thought of a young girl my age had such great needs, and that her family did not recognize these needs. They did not see her singing talent and they did not understand that she needed encouragement; Mary Fabian could sing in front of an audience and move them with her deep colorful voice. But her teeth were her greatest holdback. She dared not smile or laugh without covering her mouth with her hand. Her clothes were frumpish and did not fit well. I do believe that she and her two other sisters shared the same wardrobe. Nothing that she wore could she claim as her very own. As much as we cared for and liked each other, our friendship broke up over an incident, which now, as I look back in retrospect could have been overlooked on my part. It might not have been unavoidable but it could have been understood.

The incident was a misunderstanding over a strain of words between my mother and hers. The two mothers, hers and mine had met each other on two different occasions on the street when both were shopping on Prospect Ave. They never visited each other in their homes but Mary was in and out of our home until we both turned eighteen. Our birthdays occurred in the same month of January, and our mothers allowed us both to wear our first black dresses. We invited Mary to visit our church but she declined, stating she was a catholic and was satisfied with her own religion, but this did not change our mutual friendship. We included Mary in our parties and get togethers with our church friends. We talked and planned what we would do when we got out of High School. I wanted to go on to Cooper Union for Art courses. She wanted to pursue a singing career but it seemed to be out of the question for her. Her parents wanted her to go to nursing school, and she passed the entrance exam for Montifiorie Nurses Training School in the Bronx.

One day Mary Fabian and Mama had a conversation about the ages of her sisters and brothers. It was an innocent conversation. I know now that my mother was only questioning out of friendly interest. But her mother took great offence. One day when Jeanie and I went up to her apartment on a Saturday to take her with us on the Avenue, her mother met us at the door with an ugly scowl on her face. We made our way through the dark cluttered hallway to the steaming kitchen where her mother was cooking something green in a big pot, and boiling grey laundry in another cauldron.

She started at me immediately. Her eyes were wide and leering, beads of perspiration lined her top lip. "I don't like your mutters questions," she stated. Her hands balled up into tight fists on both hips. "She don't know how to mind her own business," her voice rose in a West Indian lilt. "Too nosey," "Humph," "Don't need to know my business, and I no like it." She spun around and pointed directly at me, "you go back home and tell you mudder to ask no questions and I tell her no lies." I looked at Mary who was now fidgeting, pushing her blouse deep in her skirt band. It was evident that she was surprised and upset at her mother for jumping at Jeanie and I. But I was very hurt that she took my mother's friendly questions home to her mother and presented it as nosey gossip. It took me no time to gather my wits about me. "Come on Jeanie," I whispered between clenched teeth. "I don't believe what I'm hearing." I saw Mary Fabian on several occasions after that. I felt I could never trust her again, and if you had lost trust in someone they couldn't be your best friend. Her mother was a bitter hostile woman with a few skeletons in her closet. I learned later that her eldest daughter was born before she was married. What a pity that the lady thought we were prying when we were not.

We were out the door and down the steps before Mary could respond. When we heard the door close behind us and the lock click clock, we realized that this was the end of our friendship. I saw her often up and down the Avenue. We spoke to each other but casually. She was always by herself and she had a sad lonely look about her. The last news I heard of her, because she was in some of the classes in High School that my other friends were in, was that Mary was going to the Dentist and had enrolled in Nursing School.

My Art Teachers in Morris High School offered me a chance to win a scholarship to Cooper Union. Some of my work was on display in the Show Windows of the Sacks Department Store on Third Ave in the Bronx. I had on display "Birds In Flight," done in bronze stippling with wings outstretched. "Listening," was another one of my presentations, done in charcoal on white gravel paper. I loved art and enjoyed dabbling in oils, but my favorite medium was black ink using fine lines.

Daddy was not agreeable about me going to Art School. He was not a worldly man, but he was living in a world that he knew well. He knew the disappointments would come in the outside world and he did not want that for his little girl at this time in her life. He was being a protective father. He did not want me to get mixed up in the Artsy crowd in the Village. He was familiar with China Town and the Village having been a Cab Drive in the City. He knew the atmosphere of the area, and worried that I might visit this Artsy town after classes. He wanted no such involvement for his daughter so he had to voice his feelings about the matter.

Somehow I was not upset when Daddy decided for me. Children usually listened to their parents back then with little chiding. "Learn how to earn a dollar," he admonished, "and learn to save half of it," and never spend your last dime. That was the end of the Art school question, and never did I feel cheated. In fact I looked forward to my first job offered to me after graduation. It was a simple small paying position in a loft in mid Manhattan working with a company of German refugees decorating children's toys.

Just as I was about to graduate from Morris High School I met Sam. I met him on a church picnic, on a hot summer's day on Aug 24, 1946. I am running ahead of my story now, but the memory of this event is etched so clearly in my mind, along with all the other most memorable dates in the Interim of my Life.

The Interim is but one link in the chain of my life. This link between my past and my future was not very strong. When I scrutinize it now more closely, I can see how vulnerable I was at the time. I was always looking and searching, but for what I really did not know. There was no special turbulence in my life at the time but there was a certain kitten like curiosity about me. I did not feel it myself, but Mama and Daddy were alert to my ever-changing personality. One week I wanted to remain alone with my books and my Bible, and on other occasions I was sharp and witty in the company of my girlfriends. I was not fresh or arrogant with my parents just changing. They knowing that all this soon would pass were very patient and watchful.

I had a good religious foundation. I had a personal relationship with my Savior Jesus Christ. But I was young, still in my teens, but I had met someone that would soon take my life over completely, although I was not aware of it at the time. Mama was familiar with my every activity. She pretended to be disinterested but was always listening and watchful. Daddy allowed Mama to handle this phase of our lives independently, that is Jeanie's and mine; and I am sure they discussed us quietly in the shadows of Mama's room after we had all said good night. Sometimes Daddy became involved when something important had to be resolved, but generally speaking Mama was the rulebook by which we had to measure up to; and as I look back now I understood that Mama had appointed herself the guardian of our days and the watchword of our ways.

One night when Jeanie and I were both still in our teen years, and I still in High School, Jeanie became very ill. We were both sleeping in our bedroom; at least I was sound asleep. Mama must have gotten up to go to the bathroom, and tiptoed by our bedroom door, which we always left open at night. Mama said she heard low moans and restless breathing. She came quickly in and found Jeanie drenched in perspiration and with shallow quick respirations. We had no telephone at the time; few families did in those post war days. Daddy went across the street to the Police Call Box and called for an ambulance. They were on the scene in a matter of minutes. Upstairs Mama was cutting Jeanie's pajamas away from her limp body. I awoke to find all this confusion about me. Jeanie appeared very sick and was barely responding. They worked quickly. Mama was calm but I heard her soft prayerful utterances as she worked over Jeanie. "Help now dear Father," Jesus! please help us now," she repeated over and over again drying off Jeanie's damp torso, arms and legs with her torn pajama pants. Jeanie had suffered some sort of cardiac failure. I did not know then just what type of heart problem it was or what precipitated it at the time. Later in years when I pursued my most important life's work, Nursing, I understood.

Jeanie was suffering from acute Congestive Heart Failure complicated by pneumonia. I will not soon forget that scene. They wrapped Jeanie up in our bed sheets and the grey ambulance blanket. And the Ambulance attendance and Daddy carried Jeanie down and out to the waiting Ambulance. The police arrived and said they had called ahead and the hospital was waiting for her. I was left alone in the apartment.

I looked at the white kitchen clock when I went to get a drink of water. It was saying 3:15 AM in the morning. I could not go back sleep. I prayed silently in my heart not even moving my lips. I knew God understood the anguish I felt for my sister, I understood that Jeanie was seriously ill. Our bedroom looked as if a tornado had hit it. The bedclothes were pulled off the bed. Our books had been knocked off the desk. I began humming "What a friend we have in Jesus" as I started to put things back in order.

CHAPTER SIX

The Driving Force

Jeanie made a remarkable recovery. She was out of the hospital in a matter of three weeks. But she was a different Jeanie. She was quiet and subdued. She was very pensive and did not laugh so readily as before she became ill. I noticed this but did not mention it to anyone.

We attended church together every Sunday and during the week to the Young Peoples' services. Mama came on Sunday mornings dressed in her purple-laced dress and wide brimmed hats. Daddy went also to our Church on Prospect Ave. He upon returning home from church walking fast, taking big strides ahead of us, he'd open the apartment door ahead of us, leave it ajar and go into his small room and there he'd stay until dinner time. Daddy was becoming very reclusive now. A young man not quite fifty years old, he was always neatly dressed. He took good care of his clothes and belongings. He had a book shelf in a corner by the one narrow window in that room. His books were lined up according to subjects. He had a big map on the wall in back of his bed. In the corner were standing, rolled up window shades with Daddy's Bible lessons which he had printed in black and red ink. Daddy was want to "Give the Lesson" on occasion on a Friday night when our minister would take a rest. Daddy was not a Deacon, not even considered an Elder in the church. But he always sat with the five or six old men on the front pews. He had an intelligent mind. He knew the Bible well and could expound on the scriptures with the best of them. Our minister recognized this and gave him every opportunity to "bring the message." He did not want publicity he didn't want to be in the limelight. He only wanted to fill in the gap and so he did from time to time.

Jeanie had lost a lot of time from High School now and showed no interest in ever returning back to finish her studies. I was now in my senior year and that would have placed Jeanie and I in the same grade although in a different school, I think

Jeanie found this to be quite distasteful and embarrassing for her as she was a much older student due to the time lost from her sickness and recuperation. No one forced or cajoled her to return to school. She seemed content to stay at home free from any classroom stress.

I was enjoying my High School days in Morris High School. Everything seemed to be coming up roses. The Post war days were upon us. Women were now in jobs that were usually filled by men. There was more food on the shelves in the store now. More oil for cars and more cars being manufactured. The wheels of recovery were turning. Recovery was the new Driving Force in the world. Recovery from the devastation that ripped through the European countries. Recovery from hatred and bloodshed. Peace was the watchword. World leaders were coming together, sitting around conference tables making Peace Treaties. Would there be peace? Who could tell? Certainly not a little family of four in the Bronx back then in the post war days.

Our Driving Force was Jesus Christ. He was the one that kept our little family together during the lean depression days. God was our champion during those infamous war years and He it was, God that kept the bloody conflict away from our continent & community. I felt the driving force within me everyday. I knew the strength and the power of Jesus Christ was what I needed everyday to keep me going. I knew it was what kept Jeanie in reasonable health, put the roses back in her cheeks, a smile on her face, a laugh in her voice and I was grateful. As Jeanie's health improved she became more active, and took more notice of me, and did not regard me as her little sister. She wanted to include me in all her plans and activities. Also Mama expected us to go everywhere together. We rode the subway together going to Brooklyn on a Saturday morning to visit Aunt Bertie and Uncle Robert. Aunt Bertie was Mama's older sister, who could almost pass for her twin. They had the same voice and carriage although I must say Auntie B was quite jovial in her jokes and quick wit, whereas Mama was a quiet stream in spirit and straight laced in character. Uncle Robert was a happy-go-lucky-rotund kind of fellow. Unlike father in a hundred ways but none the less just as true blue in words and deeds. His only aim in life was to answer Aunt Bertie's beck and call, and to allow her to win the argument that he had already precipitated between them just for the sport of teasing. She always accused "Rob" as she called him for having a lady friend on the side. This was always the ingredients and the meat of their disputes. If he came home too late from his job in the city as a storeroom man in a Man's Haberdashery, it was because of one of his "lady friends." If he left too early in the AM for his job, it was according to Auntie B to meet up with "her." Nonetheless these little squabbles did not part them and they lived together in their little upstairs Brooklyn flat for fifty years or so when the departing angel said it was enough. Aunt Bertie and Uncle Robert enjoyed our visits as much as we enjoyed visiting. They had a son name Willie whom as they said was floating around somewhere in Brooklyn, who only visited them occasionally, but this did not seem to disturb their tranquility of spirits since they were bound together in each other. It never occurred to them that things never stay the same. That time makes changes and separation is inevitable.

They were always waiting for us at the top of the stairs, when they heard their downstairs bell ring. Inside it was dimly lit, but warm and cozy. There was always cookies and hot chocolate waiting for Jeanie and I. Great pieces of pastries that Uncle Robert brought home every night from visiting the odd little bakeshops in the city. After kisses were exchanged her first question was "Is Mother alright," she called our Mama "Mother", trying to be real proper as she thought our Mama was "I know," she answered her own question with a flick of the wrist "She's home cleaning the house." "Why doesn't she let that little place stink itself up," she would say winking at Rob. "She thinks she's living in the Queens Castle, and she always broadened her A's when mentioning Castle. Thusly our visits begun.

They had a dusty old spare room off from their green bedroom. They let us rummage through boxes and bags of stuff that they had allowed to accumulate just for the occasion. Jeanie always found pieces of lace and feathers that she promised to use for her hats and dresses. I was mostly interested in the old faded photo albums and Aunt Bertie always had a story connected with each old photo. Her trunks were packed with dusty old books, of poems, prose and novels; which contented me for hours. I stretched out on her green counterpane, thumbing through these raggedy old volumes while Jeanie delighted herself among the souvenirs of the past.

They loaded us up with pieces of ham and cheese and slices of cake for Mama and Daddy. They gave us our carfare back to the Bronx, even though they knew we already had it. We started back before three in the afternoon. I carried mostly all the packages, not wanting to tire Jeanie out, but she seemed to enjoy the excursion at least once a month, and did not seem any worse for it. Nonetheless, Jeanie became everyone's concern. Even though she never verbalized any discomfort, all our activities were planned around Jeanie. She never returned to Jane Adams H.S. to finish her last year and no one broached the subject to her. We now moved from the third floor apartment to a first floor apartment so that Jeanie had only one short flight of steps to climb. The move was in the front of the same building. Our bedroom and Mama's bedroom faced the street. There was and extra small bedroom off the living room that looked out to the back courtyard. We were now in five rooms and they did not run behind the other. The kitchen was cozy and square with large wooden cabinets from floor to ceiling. We now had a gas stove; it was black and white and had a double oven standing on top of each other. Daddy replaced the old wooden icebox with a shiny new Westinghouse refrigerator. Things were looking up. We were beginning to modernize. We kept the old Settee and armchair, but added some new lamps that Daddy claimed he stumbled on in a lighting shop on the East Side. Mama put up new lace curtains to the front windows and to the French doors that opened up from the living room into Mama's bedroom. We called it Mama's bedroom now because Daddy had moved a pullout bed along with his sewing machine into the little extra room off from the Living room. Our bedroom, Jeanie's and mine was to the left of Mama's. Mama allowed us to decorate and fix up our room the way we wanted it.

Jeanie had so many clothes. Hats and shoes and bags and accessories. It seemed her clothes were everywhere. I made it my job to keep all our belongings neat and orderly. I did all the dusting and sweeping for the two of us. I did not mind, I did not want Jeanie to exert herself after all she was being kept from school to recuperate. Mama took her back to the clinic for check-ups once a month. She's coming alone fine, the Doctor said. Don't let her over-do, don't let her catch colds, and thus we watched her like a hawk. Jeanie was beginning to glow. She started to gain her strength back. She didn't seem breathless when walking. Her appetite was good and she was gaining back the weight she had lost. She became her jovial self. Mama was joyful for God was answering her prayers and Jeanie was beginning to look like her old self.

One by one our soldiers returned home from overseas. Ronald was stationed in Guam with the new Peace keeping forces. Jeanie was receiving letters every week from him now. He had admired Jeanie a short while back when we all sang together in the youth group in our church. He could not for get her eyes, he stated. He loved her beautiful smile. His letters were sprinkled with love verses. Was he serious? Jeanie could not tell but she certainly was interested and flattered. She let me read her mail. She enjoyed reading these letters and looked forward to receiving them but did not know how to answer them. I began answering Jeanie's letters to Ronald for her and she copied them over in her flourishing script. She would perfume the envelopes with her favorite Blue Grass scent and print on the back flap of the envelope SWAK sealed with a kiss.

A year had passed now since Jeanie had became ill and seemed fully recovered. She began helping Mama around the house. She loved to cook and took over some of the kitchen chores. This allowed Mama the time to take in little ones for working mothers. She was now caring for two little sisters from across the street and a sweet little chubby boy named Barry who needed desperately to be potty trained, which Mama started almost immediately and fully accomplished in a matter of two weeks.

In the meantime Daddy had been transferred from his Red Capping job to a Board Room Attendant in the New York Central Railroad System. His duties were now very different from toting baggage on and off the trains at the Grand Central Station as it was called then before it became the Pen Central System. He had a nine to five job on one of the higher floors. He wore a suit and tie very day and had his own desk and typewriter outside of the boardroom. The boardroom as he explained it was where all the big decisions had to be made by the big wigs of the New York Central Systems. He was responsible for all the Literature, mail, outgoing and incoming. He answered the telephones and was responsible for maintaining and securing the secret votes of the stockholders present. He had to collect and lock away all the proxies of the stockholders not present. But Daddy remained the same and never changed neither in personality or pride. I understood years later that it was beneficial for the N.Y. Central System to hire a man of color to fill a position of a boardroom attendant. A young college fellow fresh out of school applied for the job, but it was to the systems advantage to take one of the boys from the "Lower Level" and bring him upstairs. The lower level was a real place in the Railroad Terminal. It was a dark sweaty tunnel where the Negro Red Caps chased down the passengers swarming from the incoming trains. Grabbing their baggage they would run ahead to the waiting cabs, on the busy 42nd St. street curbs; fling open the doors of the taxies' for their patrons, load their baggage in the trunk and wave the driver on with a salute. This was truly a lower level job. But Daddy did his job well. He was cautious, prompt and of a quiet spirit. He was not loud and raucous, but always correct and fair in all his dealings. Handsome, clean cut, and well mannered, he fit the bill. So it was he who was elevated to higher ground. Daddy stayed with the New York Central System for 25 years and was given a golden Railroad nail and a gold watch upon retirement.

Jeanie never returned to school. She finally took a job with the Simplicity

Pattern Company, folding patterns. She seemed to enjoy her work immensely. She was able to get free patterns she gleaned new ideas for styles, and she now had her own pocket money. Salaries were small in those days, but she made enough to help me through my high school days. Jeanie was not a selfish girl. When she bought for herself she always bought for Mama and me. But the job did not last long, it folded up in six months time. But Jeanie was lucky and blessed, she soon found another job to her liking as she so stated. It was the Jaubert Ce' Perfume Factory, housed in a brand new White Plant on Prospect Ave in walking distance from our home. She worked here for another six months before it moved to another location. She managed to save a few dollars squirreling away a few dollars each week under her lacy garments in the middle drawer of our wooden highboy.

After the exchange of many letters and pictures, Ronald wrote that he was coming home. What a flurry and a dither Jeanie was in. She had little time to get herself ready for the event. He was expected by the end of Sept in 1946. She had at the most six weeks to ready herself. That summer of 1946 was very eventful for both Jeanie and I. That year I met Sam at our church picnic and Jeanie's soldier boy came home. Did Mama know? How could she know, that she was to lose both her daughters who she loved dearer than life itself to these two young men.

CHAPTER SEVEN

Days of Hearts and Roses

Sometimes one day in our lives can change the course of our future. Up until this present time, I was a carefree young woman with no special plans for the future, but to graduate from High School and to work at my job appointed for me by the Art Instructor in Morris High School.

The Carol Drug Supply Co. on East 23rd Street was looking for a bight young artist willing to learn the hand decorating business. My art instructor thought I was that bright young person they were looking for. I was elected Class Artist of my graduating class, and my picture in the year book with my art pallet and brushes attested to this fact. I had won this title of "Class Artist" over two other contestants who were trying for the same honors.

Jeanie was well now for sure and actively planning her future around Ronald. I was not attracted to anyone at that time. I was happy and carefree looking forward to graduation and my new job. Now and then our cousins visited us from my parents' homeland Bermuda. The two cousins who came most often to visit us were sisters, Endera and Mary. Their mother and my mother, and Aunt Bertie were sisters. Endera took a special liking to me, and promised if I ever got married that she would be under my elbow to help dress me for the occasion. But I loved Mary dearly and did not feel it unfair to show preferences between cousins. These two sisters Endera and Mary were the exact opposite of each other. Endera was quite greedy in character and always looking for some personal gain in everything she did and said. She was married to Maxwell, a tolerant man and as docile as a lamb. He was a heavy built man with a generous heart to match, always reaching in his pockets ready to pay for whatever Endera's heart fancied. Endera was ten years older than myself but yet could not understand that folks living in the U.S. were not all rich with bulging pockets. Mary was of a quieter sweeter spirit. Looking to visit Aunt Bertie and to be of help to anyone she encountered. Mary loved to read her Bible and encouraged me to memorize Bible verses. Mary was not married, and had stated that she had planned one time in earlier days to marry but had been disappointed. She did not elaborate, but I could sense the sadness in her voice. When these two young ladies and Maxwell visited they usually stayed between our house and Aunt Bertie's apartment. They loved the city and visited places of interest that I living here in the city had not seen. Soon Endera would become homesick for her beautiful Island of Bermuda and Maxwell would have to cut their visit short, and practically carry her prostrate onto the waiting plane. We all knew she was spoiled, could not help herself, and Maxwell added to the calamity of the situation. Mary usually stayed on with us after her sister and husband left to go back home. I enjoyed the few quiet days that Mary Jean and I had together without the hustle and bustle of touring the city. Nonetheless we were cousins and the bloodlines restrained Jeanie and I from showing any partiality between the two sisters.

Mama was kept quite busy intermittently between these visits from Bermuda and the care of the little ones that the working mothers in the neighborhood placed in her charge.

Jeanie and I had not really planned to go to our church picnic in Cunningham Park. It just happened that way; we both got up early and saw that the weather was right and started on our way. We threw some sandwiches together made from canned ham, dressed with mustard and mayonnaise, added some apples and cookies. We mixed up some lemon and ice chunks. We grabbed the old picnic basket and were around the corner to our church to wait with the gathering crowd of young people waiting for the bus that would take us to the picnic grounds. Believe it or not we arrived just in time, the bus pulled up in a matter of minutes.

We had a great time at the picnic. This is the one day in my life that made the difference in my future. Years later, I would often sit and wonder, what if? What if I had not gone to the picnic? What if Jeanie and I did not take that little small insignificant lunch and share it with that certain someone? What if I hadn't been so friendly and forward with that certain someone?

The weather was warm and balmy that day. Jeanie and I knew everyone there. My girlfriend Cindy had come on our church bus also. In fact there were three church groups on the picnic grounds that day. We ate some of our lunch in the first two hours, covered the rest over, and then ambled down to the ball park to watch the games. Jeanie had her camera with her and she was quick with the shutters. A baseball game was in progress between two of the church groups. The girls were sitting around in little bunches on the ground, handing out cool drinks to the fellows playing baseball between games. We laughed and joked and compared the guys to each other, the way young girls have since the beginning of time. Jeanie must have taken over a dozen pictures that day. There was a lot of hand clapping screaming and routing for their own team and all in shear fun. There were no rewards or prizes given out to the winning team, just exhilaration and elation expressed among young people having a little bit of fun and recreation before the start of the hard serious days of everyday living.

From the games we moved to the swings and seesaws. The fellows came over to push the girls on the swings and bump them on the seesaws. But I did not want to be pushed in my swing. It all seemed like good carefree fun but I didn't seem to be able to loosen myself up enough to get involved in the frolicking. But before I could think twice, someone was behind me pushing me in my swing with all his might. Jeanie was quick with her camera taking snaps of this change of events. Everyone was laughing, and posing for Jeanie. No one else thought to bring along his or her camera. We'll have some really good snaps she kept saying. To remember this day, she said winking my way. From the swings we found our way to the lunch tables again. We had a little leftover lunch just a few pieces of fruit and a couple of wrinkled up sandwiches. Cindy my school pal at the time who attended one of the invited churches hung around our table with Jeanie and I. I was glad for the shady tree branches hanging over our table and benches. It was a relief to feel the cool breezes fanning our hot faces after the fun and games. Cindy and I sat down heavily on one of the benches. She opened the front of her blouse and started to fan her neck and face rapidly. I lifted my long unkempt hair over my head and started fanning the back of my neck. Jeanie started to pour out the rest of the Kool-Aid into the paper cups we had brought along. I felt some quiet footsteps tip-toeing behind me. I turned quickly. There was this bold overbearing young man standing behind me. "I'm hungry he said, smiling and showing a wide grin and white even teeth." "I don't have anything to eat, and I don't even have a table of my own." "Whom did you come with?" I asked. He hung his head sheepishly. "I'm alone, and I'm lonely," he said. "May I sit down and have something to drink?" He looked in Jeanie's direction and at the filled paper cups. I said to myself. A hungry man could not shout that loud with the vim and vigor of the umpire, that he was at the ball game. He certainly has been well fed up until now I thought to myself. While I hesitated to speak again, Jeanie had found two wrinkled up sandwiches, placed them on a napkin and a cup of Kool-Aid on the table in front of him. He wolfed if down in two minutes and wiped his mouth on his rolled up sleeves. Jeanie was now bouncing around again with her camera, she seemed possessed. "Let me take your picture" she called out to the umpire. "I want to send a picture of a hungry man to the newspaper," she went on laughing at her own joke.

I glanced over the hungry young man. He was young although not as young as myself but I noticed a fun twinkle in his eyes. And he certainly was not malnutrition; in fact he was well built and stocky. I cannot comprehend now, as I look back on one short split second in my life, how I lost my wits, or what drove me to pose for a picture with this new comer and I didn't even know his name. He jumped up quickly from the table and squatted on the grass, a few feet away from the benches. He looked as if he was getting ready to play baseball all over again and about to call out BALL I OR BALL II but instead he grinned back at Jeanie waiting for her to say cheese. In a flash I hopped over to him and perched myself uninvited on his one folded knee and smiled for Jeanie's camera. Yes, that's just what I did. I posed unabashed with a tight grip around his neck, while his knees did a trembly jig underneath the weight of my body. The die was then cast forever.

After the picture taking episode, we cleared away our table and trudged over to the Park's Rest rooms. The buses were scheduled to leave at six p.m. We had to be at the Bus Loading zone before then. I followed Jeanie and Cindy along with the other girls in our group to the Ladies Rest room. The place was crowded and noisy. We had to wait in line. Jeanie decided she had to comb out her hair at the mirrors over the sinks. She had to look pretty at all times regardless of where she was. I thought to myself she's thinking of Ronald. Just in case he pops up somewhere unannounced, she'll be neat as a pin.

I also glanced at myself in the mirror while waiting my turn in line. I looked disheveled and sunburned like a salmon. I had not put any color to my lips or cheeks. There was none needed. My lose course hair was hanging limp around my face and shoulders without any shape or style. Well I thought to myself, anyone could see I've been out in the Wilds today.

Having finished our business in the little girls' room, we made it back to the Bus depot just in time. Everyone was waving goodbyes' and throwing kisses to each other. These were good friendly times. We had church picnics about two or three times during the summer season. We always sang our hymns and choruses in the buses going home. Cindy and I would really now have something to whisper and muddle over when we would meet after church services. She did not have a steady beau but was always looking and hoping for someone to notice her. Cindy was pretty with a round baby doll face. A pleasing smile and a classy figure, Cindy was a leader and whoever was her friend understood she led the way in almost every circumstance. But somehow she could not lead me, one way or the other. I appreciated her company, enjoyed our mutual jokes and secrets together, but she really was not my bosom friend. I had been down that road before, so it's easy to say that Cindy and I complimented each other. She understood that I did not need to be led by her, and she knew she could not impress me. We were just mutual buddies.

There were not too many seats left on the bus. Jeanie sat in front of me with one of her friends. Cindy and I sat directly in back. A few more strugglers made it on the bus and the seats were all soon taken up. Some had to stand in the center of the bus, swinging and swaying by the hand holders. We started home a little after six thirty P.M. The Bus driver wanted to be sure we had everyone. Someone started up a song and soon everyone was clapping and singing to "On The Homeward Way With The King." "On The Blessed Homeward Way." That was always the song we song when coming home from a church picnic in those early carefree days. That was the homebound song.

I looked up and noticed the hungry young fellow with the wide grin was hovering over me, hanging by the hand holders and intently watching me. "Can I sit next to you," he said in a wimpy voice. I stared back at him in disbelief. How could he expect to sit next to me when Cindy was already sitting there? I whispered to Cindy "don't you dare to move from this seat." "I'm all alone," he teased over and over again. "I need some company." "Don't you feel sorry for me?" Indeed he had no picnic bag nor knapsack as some of the other fellows had. I wondered to myself, he does seem to be a loner. I looked up at him and said. "I tell you what; you can have the picture we took together when Jeanie gets the pictures developed. I didn't know when or where I would see him again and it really didn't matter. I was only concerned with curbing his intentions.

The bus was now bumping along the main highway leading to the Bronx. Everyone was merry and singing. My lonely buddy was pretending to stumble and lose balance. Suddenly a light switched on in my head. "Jeanie" I said you do have the camera don't you?" Jeanie paused a short moment. Her mouth flew open. "Oh my Gosh," she exclaimed. She searched frantically in the bag on her lap. "Oh my" "How could I?" I left it on the sink in the Park's Rest room.

I was in limbo the next few weeks that followed the picnic. I was afflicted with a very annoying and unsightly skin rash. I had a low grade temperature and was itching all over my face, neck, and arms. Sis Marvin a nurse in our church put me to bed and bathed me in sterile water and calamine lotion. She said I had ragweed fever. The summer was waning and after spending three days in bed I sat in our bedroom window all painted up with calamine lotion; watching the Bike races go by. This event always ended the summer season's activities in the Bronx. I watched dreamful with chin in cupped hand as the different colored "Two Wheelers," as they called them whirled up and down in and out of our noisy street. After about a week of weakness and lethargy I decided to shake myself and attend the youth meeting with Jeanie at our church on the last Saturday evening in August. The church was crowded with young people singing and clapping. These were happy times for us. We enjoyed our religion and ourselves. I loved Jesus my Lord and Savior and always felt at home when inside the walls of our House of Worship. We sang all the new choruses, some learned from the "Jack Wurtson Campaign. One of my favorites was "Child of the King." This hymn always gave me a lift. I recognized at a very young age that I was a spiritually rich person. My parents were not rich and had very few worldly possessions, but I had an abiding faith in god. I knew that my heavenly father was the King of the Universe, and no good thing would he withhold from those who would walk upright before him. Yes Jesus Christ was my heavenly Father and I was child of The King.

When the church service was over just a little after 10 P.M., Jeanie and I decided to walk home, just a short block and a half around the corner. Who should jump in front of us? elf like, and with innocent smiles; but the Ball Park Umpire? We both said "Hi" in unison and surprise. At least Jeanie and I were very surprised, but it seemed to me this was one of his best laid out plans. "I found out where you two cuties live," he grinned. "They told me," he exclaimed pointing to the young folks milling around the church entrance; and I also saw you in the window when I rode through on my bike, a few days back. He laughed loudly and slapped his thighs, "I saw you with all that white stuff on your face." "Girlie it's too early for Halloween."

He really was funny and he did make me laugh. "I am walking you to your door, he said looking directly at me. He did not look at Jeanie. He took my arm persistently and led me down the street. At the doorstep of our house, we paused, and he told me his full name, where he lived, and promised I would see him again. He was short with a stocky build and had an interesting face. I was not sure about him or even if I welcomed his interests. But he made sure that I did see him again. Jeanie's Ronald soon came home from the Army and she introduced him to Sam, the Ball Park Umpire.

Soon Jeanie and Ronald, Sam and I began going everywhere together. Jeanie was delirious; she seemed to be walking on clouds. Ronald brought her many little gifts of endearments. She hung onto his every word and he was very demonstrative with his attentions. Ronald called Jeanie his Glamour Queen, and indeed she had gone to great lengths to make herself attractive to her homecoming soldier boy. They saw each other at least three times a week. He would come out and sit on the couch with Jeanie talking and laughing until late in the evening. Then Daddy would come out of his room, clear his throat, piddle around in the kitchen, signaling it was time for him to leave.

Sam showed up at our church every Sunday morning dressed in his modified Zoot Suit, and shiny pointed toe shoes as he stated were so crafted to kill roaches in corners. He never looked hungry or starved as he first professed to be, and he did wear the latest styles of the day. Every wavy strand of his hair was in place laid down by "Murray's Hair grease and water. He said he was George Raft's rival and I was impressed. He said that he was "sharp as a pin" and had a "neat pleat" which was the vernacular of the day meaning he was a well dressed man. Back then the young men took pride in their attire or else they were in one of "Uncle Sam's Uniform. There was something new and different about this man who was a few years my senior. He was bewitching and compelling and I began to look forward to seeing him in church. Mama saw him from her front window when he walked me home from church. Mama did not attend services as she used to do, often complaining of tiredness and episodes of heat flushes and chills. She said she did not want to be embarrassed when her face turned suddenly beet red. In those days women usually suffered through those trying days in silence not seeking any kind of emotional or medical relief. They sometimes named the problem something other than what it really was.

One Sunday Sam came up the one flight of steps in our apartment building to meet Mama. He wanted to take me out on a date and I wanted to go out with him; but I felt he had to come to my home and meet my mother and ask her permission first. This he did and Mama responded favorably. I was surprised she offered not opposition.

Everything was running along smoothly. I was back in school in the last half of my last year in High school looking forward to graduation. Jeanie and Ronald were inseparable. It was clear that they were in love. Was there a wedding plan in the future for them? Jeanie hinted that this was so. Jeanie was looking at Bridal gowns in newspapers and magazines. Mama and Daddy both joked with Ronald. They made him feel at home. Mama always kept chilled fruit in the fridge that Jeanie could serve to him when he came by. In the meantime Sam and I became a real couple and we did everything together and I was never without an escort. I was quite flattered at the time at the attention that this new man in my life Sam Green was affording me, and I did not understand that he was very serious about our relationship. One day someone whispered some ugly gossip to Mama about Sam. They said he was too fast, too old for me and a man about town. Whatever that all meant I did not know, I was bewildered. Mama forbade me to see him again because as she said he was not good for me.

Soon Christmas time rolled around and Ronald gave Jeanie an engagement ring for Christmas. She was both elated and speechless. Aunt Bertie and Uncle Robert arrived on the scene soon after Jeanie called them at the corner Drug store to tell them the news of the engagement. Aunt Bertie had to examine the ring to check its worth. She held it up high to the kitchen light and blew a couple of deep puff under the diamond setting. "Yes," she said, "It does have a faint whistle and quite a few prisms." She turned it over and over in the palm of her hand and rubbed it on the sleeve of her blouse much to Jeanie's consternation. "Should have been a larger stone," she said giving it back to Jeanie, "but it's a real diamond." My niece deserves a bigger stone than that little dew-drop. Jeanie knew that if the ring did not pass Aunt Bertie's inspection. She would have said, "Humph and Mama and Auntie B would have said nothing at all nudging elbows. But this was not the case. The ring passed the test and Jeanie felt proud.

Although Mama had told me not to see Sam Green anymore, she knew he came to our church, and she allowed him to visit us at Christmas. He came the Day before Christmas with gifts for Mama, Daddy and Jeanie. My gift was a beautiful gold bracelet. Time was flying past us now. Time, time, why in such a hurry. I saw old man Time with wings on his feet. The end of the year was fast approaching. The design in the Tapestry was becoming clear, the colors more profuse and I had a few anxious feelings behind all this gaiety.

Jeanie was wearing Ronald's ring, but there were no plans in progress. No one was engaged for long periods of time back then. They were together but he seemed to be hesitant, Jeanie said, "We just need a little more time to be sure." I thought to myself that all the sureness should be figured out before the ring. Mama continued to show Sam a certain coldness. She seemed to know something I didn't know. Then Jeanie laughed good-naturedly, maybe we'll wait for you and Sam so we could have a double wedding. I made no comment. I was only interested in my sister's future at this point.

Mama did not want Sam near me on the day of my graduation from High School. But he sent me a beautiful bouquet of flowers which I though it very sweet of him to do so. He seemed to know all the right things to do on any given occasion. Mama said she was going to trust me to go back and forth to my Artist joy in the city and not to involve myself with Sam. But soon he learned from Ronald just where I worked and would escort me home from my job on the subway and delivers me safe and sound every evening on my doorstep. Mama soon relented and was thankful that her daughter was home safe every evening.

The four of us, Jeanie and Ronald, Sam and I began dating together. Mama seemed not to mind or else she made up her mind not to let it bother her that her younger daughter was in the company of someone she didn't approve of. Ronald and Sam soon became fast friends. They seemed to always have something to talk about privately. They were real buddies. Jeanie and I also became closer than ever; we were more than sisters, we were each other's confidants. One day she confided that she felt that Ronald was now stalling concerning the wedding plans. She still wore his engagement ring, but felt closer to him before the engagement than she did after receiving the ring. I watched the two of them together. He always seemed so gallant, his hand always at her elbow when guiding her in the streets; her chair pulled out appropriately when being seated in a restaurant, still the love light in their eyes, was it veiled?

On one occasion we were having supper out, seated a dimly late table, and Ronald suddenly remembered a very important call he had to make. He kissed Jeanie on the forehead, excused himself and never returned back to the table. How embarrassed Jeanie was. But he had an excuse for Jeanie. He was so sweet and apologetic, claiming he felt ill and did not want her to see him so. On another occasion we were coming home in a taxi, when he asked Sam to see Jeanie home along with me, as he suddenly remembered that he had to see an old army buddy who lived in the next block. Now at this point Jeanie was beginning to get the message. She really could not count on him for much wedding plans. When he was with her, he protested his love for her and made her feel like a princess. "But he's not stead," she confided. "I think he keeping something from me." And indeed he was keeping his real self in hiding. He was hiding behind a facade of chivalry. Thinking his engagement to Jeanie "was the right thing to do," since she was so faithful to him while he was away in the Army. He believed the engagement to Jeanie would hide his true self and unreal lifestyle, not taking into account the damage the cover-up would did to Jeanie. He confided in Sam his real problems. He was not a real man anymore. He blamed it all on the Army. But it was clear he could never be a real husband to Jeanie. She did not know this at first, but suspicious as much later on, sensing something was very wrong with their relationship. Hew told her nothing, but tried to fade out of the picture. His visits were fewer and further apart. Mama and Daddy noticed his delinquent behavior and advised Jeanie to give back the ring and break off the engagement.

Jeanie did exactly as she was advised to do. She gave Ronald back the ring and to her surprise and bewilderment he made no protest. She told me later she expected Ronald to disagree with her decision to refuse to break up or to even ask for some more time to gather his wits about him. She asked me in the quiet of our sunlit bedroom one Sunday morning. "What does it mean when a man can't be a man anymore?" "Will he ever change?" "What did the Army do o him to make him so different?" This was a sad young woman who had staked her life and future on someone she loved dearly. I couldn't help her. I didn't know what to say to her. I tried to fill the void in her life with my company and our many girlfriends. Everyone loved Jeanie. Everyone knew something had transpired in the relationship between Jeanie and Ronald. Mama and Daddy felt they had given Jeanie the right advice. They could not allow Jeanie to string along with someone whose love was not true, and had little depth of spirit and integrity. It was clear to all that he was using Jeanie to test his strength as a real man. He had failed the test and had not enough gumption to come to her and explain his plight. He allowed her to float along with his tardy habits and questionable behavior. He was sweet and gentleman like when with her, but these times were few and could not be counted on. She had to pretend it was a small thing. He did not argue the decision so she told everyone that she was the one who had broken the engagement. Jeanie presented a very calm and casual exterior to everyone. She began to date other who were always attracted to her. One young man name Elton Galis, an organist in his church would have married Jeanie the next month if she had consented. But he was too presumptuous and bold and Jeanie said he had a bad case of B.O. We spent many a Friday or Saturday evening, sitting in Myers' Drug and Malt Shop on Prospect Ave. Here we sat and talked for hours, Jeanie, Sam and I in the dimly lit booths. Here couples mapped out their life's plans. Here love matches were made, love songs played on the jukeboxes hanging over the tables, and hearts mended over banana splits and sky scraper dips. Was Jeanie going to survive these heart rending days of her young womanhood. Her smile was bright and convincing. But no one really knew the sad songs in her heart.

CHAPTER EIGHT

Sam

I really enjoyed my artist job in the heart of New York City. I felt I was growing wings; knowing the freedom of a fledgling discovering it could actually fly after being pushed out of the nest. The money was small but the opportunity to learn all sorts of new things and experiences was at my fingertips. I was a novice and willing to learn. The first group was German artist, Herr Gorgan and his wife Frau Emma. Their studio was a small loft overlooking a very busy street in the garment district of New York City. Everyone referred to Frau Emma as a stocky woman with smiles creased all around her eyes and mouth. Her current joy was to have me in her hands so that she could mold me as she said and bring out the best in me. She said she recognized my potential. I enjoyed the long talks we had together in the morning when I would arrive earlier than the other girls. She would talk about her native Germany. How she loved her country, how she was sorry for her people, who allowed such a Devil as Hitler to come in and spread his ominous propaganda over Europe. She sighed tearfully when she realized that she, Herr Borgan and their grown son Eric had left in time having not witnessed the awful atrocities enacted against the Jewish people. Two of the young women working with us were German Jews. Gerta was the eldest and was always tearful when talking about these subjects that were very painful to her. Maila Braum, a very beautiful tall and willowy German girl would always hum German songs and lullaby's when working and especially during these conversations.

Initially we decorated baby toys with sprigs of flowers, cat faces, and bunnies. I learned how to use the paintbrush freely and with a flourish. But the rose was my greatest accomplishment. I learned how to paint a rose, free hand starting from the center and by using different shades of pink tinged with white I was able to create the most exquisite piece of hand painted art. This was a learned art, and the Europeans were in possession of the hand decorating business and I did not have to go to any college to study, I just had to be a willing apprentice.

There were other jobs that I went to after my initial job. Hand painting usually is seasonal, and the Artists usually move about in a cycle finding work and new opportunities where they presented themselves. Eventually I was able to paint the head of a horse in a matter of minutes. I painted horses on ties and roses on ceramics. We also painted on ladies stockings. This was a new fad. It caught on like wildfire but was short lived.

Sam and I went to quite a few of the Art exhibits in the village, and I discovered that he enjoyed art as much as I did. In fact he was very talented in oils and especially so since he had no formal Art training whatsoever. Sam also worked in the City, met me faithfully every evening outside my job and escorted me home. Sometimes we stopped at my favorite "Chock Full O' Nuts" for coffee and donuts, before starting out on the crowded subways. Sam always said that the subway ride home was the best part of his day. The cars were so crowded and packed so tightly that I had no other alternative but to snuggle close in his protective arms. Every morning he would come down the street to my house, whistle under my bedroom window, and we would ride into the city together. He had told Mama in the very beginning that he only wanted to be with me for companionship's sake. She chuckled then, but one evening she called out the window after him when he was going up the street "Mighty long Companionship!" and he answered back with a slap on his thigh, "and it might go on forever!"

Now Mama was no dumb lady. She had not lived in this world for almost forty nine years for nothing. She recognized the persistence in his voice and in his deportment. She placed no checks next to his name upon their first meetings, and she did not go out of her way to make him comfortable when he visited our home. But she thought of him as a mail carrier. Nothing could deter him from his round of duties; which was escorting me to and from my job safely every working day, of which she was very grateful.

"How much do you care for him?" she asked me one day, "and what do you know about him?" She gazed at me with tired eyes. "Be careful Mimsie, she said, when men grow older, they grow jealous." Be very careful, and look once, twice, three times before you leap. I knew at this point what she was thinking about and how she felt. She was thinking of Jeanie and Ronald. She did not want to witness another disappointment in the life of her younger daughter. Yet she knew she had to warn, then wait it out. But I said to myself, can anyone be truly sure?" You look good, long and hard, and try to convince yourself that you will live with the Prince of your choice happily ever after.

We decided to marry. I knew that I loved this man in my life. I looked for no other, and was always happy when we were together. Sam proposed to me on a Double Decker bus on one rainy night in mid Manhattan. He always teased me later, that I was the one that proposed, but I only guided his thoughts in that direction. We were both looking out the rain spotted windows together and he spied a new 1947 car, gliding along side of the bus, and he asked me if I liked what I saw, and if I would like to have one of these new 1947 models. I spontaneously replied, "No I'd rather have you instead." Well the die was cast again, just as it was on the picnic day of our first meeting. That day without forethought I perched on his lap and posed for a picture with him. So did I now direct a new train of thought that he quickly capitalized on? The thought was not new, he had hinted before how he felt about me, but was not sure of being accepted. Sam's face was now a moonbeam, smiling from ear to ear in that dimly lit Double Decker bus on that rainy evening in mid Manhattan. He hurriedly grabbed my hand and squeezed it. "You know I'll always give you what you want; he said and I'll be less expensive than the car.

When I told Mama, she did not seem surprised. "I knew this was coming sooner or later," she said. She sounded as if she were listening to a storm warning coming over the radio. She pulled her bathrobe tighter around her waist, and sighed deeply. "I certainly have a lot to pray about now."

I do not know at this point in time how much Mama and Daddy shared with each other. I know now that Joanna and Charlie was an old fashioned couple, and like all couples they had their differences. They appeared pleasant when in company of others, but each seemed to be contented without the other. Mama loved friends and company; she was a very outgoing person, whereas Daddy was just the opposite. Her family and especially her daughters were the center of her world. She had seen the hurt in her oldest daughter's eyes, witnessed her suffering as she tried to lead a normal life, and she did not wish the same for her younger daughter. I know now that Sam was not her choice for me. He appeared to be too self sufficient and a man who had been around. But parents cannot choose for their children; but can only hope and pray the best for them. Mama had no one to talk over her misgivings with. Aunt Bertie and Uncle Robert did not visit as often as before because Uncle Robert was becoming overweight and had a raspy asthmatic cough when climbing the subway steps. This left her to brood alone with a lot of unanswered questions. Daddy was only too happy to be left out of the pictures. He made a short curt statement to Mama. "When the time comes; I know the right questions to ask him, and they'll be the most important ones. Well that closed the subject indeed. Now we soon began planning for our big day. Sam presented me with a beautiful blue white diamond soon after that rainy night on the Double Decker bus. How ironic it was, that less than a year earlier, I had spurned his attention on a picnic bus and had welcomed then on a city bus.

I fell in love with Sam's family right from the start. They were so sincere and welcomed me into their family circle. Sam had three doting sisters and three brothers. His mother was a roly-poly lady with a homey wholesome air about her. She brought her children up in the same Pentecostal faith as ours and we spent many quiet sobering talks together exploring each other's hearts. We talked about our faith in Jesus Christ and how we hoped to guide our children, hers and mine in the fear and praise of our dear Savior. I was pleased and happy and I felt I had gained a second mother, and indeed I had. She told me years later, how she loved me dearly as her own daughter, and the only difference was that she hadn't birthed me. In years to come Dear Mother, as all called her helped me raise my little ones and became my spiritual guide and confidant.

Sam came to our house on the first Sunday in June 1947 with the ring in his breast pocket. He promised he would ask my father for permission to marry me, and he did just that. Jeanie and I did not attend services that Sunday morning and I hinted to Daddy to stay at home because Sam wanted to talk with him. Mama and Daddy both dressed themselves up special and the apartment was sparkling and festive indeed. I called Daddy into the living room as soon as Sam arrived so he wouldn't have to sweat it out. Mama had a capon bird in the oven with all the trimmings and Mama and Jeanie were clanking the dishes and pots so noticeably in the kitchens.

Daddy pretended to be surprised when Sam finally cleared his throat and asked for my hand in marriage. But his face lit up like a sunbeam. He side glanced at Sam and pretended hesitation. "How old are you?" he asked point blank of Sam. I heard him swallow. "I'm twenty seven." "Do you have a Job?" was the next question, "Yes Sir I have two good jobs," was the next flat answer. Silence hung in the air, and the clatter in the kitchen had stopped, and Daddy had a twinkle in his eyes. He turned to me and questioned me. "Do you love this young man?" I gave Sam a sideways glance.

Sure do I said sheepishly, not expecting this. Daddy called out to Mama in the kitchen. She came in wiping her hands on her apron. Did you know what was going on between these two he asked? Mama's mouth flew open in disbelief. Daddy laughed a loud guffaw. Put the ring on her finger son he said, and lets get it over with I'm hungry and it sure smells good. That was the most he said at any given time at one clip, but whatever and whenever it was it was words that made good sense.

Well Sam placed the ring on my finger, and I kissed the ring and Sam square on the lips, right in front of Mama, Daddy and Jeanie and thought to myself how bold I was getting to be. The big dining room table was opened up in the center of the living room; and Mama and Jeanie had a beautiful spread prepared for us. After dinner Sam went over to the piano and started playing some tunes that he made up as he went along. My piano was not accustomed to being thumped and pounded in such a manner, but this was the prelude to another softer gentler tune "like O' Promise Me."

I was now an engaged woman at the age of nineteen years old. Sometimes I wanted to be a little girl again. I would come from work, kick off my shoes, and curl up on the foot of Mama's bed and wait to be called to supper. Mama would come tiptoeing in pull down the shades and pull the covers over me. I felt comforted and protected here under the warm covers of Mama's bed. Why did I seek protection and comfort at this time? I was not unhappy at all but uncertain. Everything was moving so fast. Time, time slow down a bit I whispered to myself. Give me a little more time. I haven't lived enough yet I felt and I am still very young. Am I doing the right thing, is it all going to turn out O.K.? These were the thought that always raced through my brain now whenever I was by myself. But time did not tarry, and days moved into weeks and months. Sam was as sweet as honey and as steady as a racehorse. We went everywhere together and was accepted as a couple. Two weeks before our wedding on Aug 8th 1948 our bands were read in church. Mama and Daddy arrived together and Jeanie was dressed tastefully. We had dinner that afternoon after church in a cozy little restaurant in Harlem. At this time we thought we were the two happiest and luckiest people in the world and we probably were at the time.

Our wedding day was ordered up just for us. Bright blue ship, clear sunshine and not too hot for a day in August. My four bridesmaids were dressed in old rose and lime green ankle length waltz gowns, with snowy white to the elbow gloves. Their wide brimmed hats matched the color of their dresses with a ribbon that tied under the chin in a wide bow. I was lucky that my bridesmaids could sew, and Jeanie helped each one with the machine stitching. We all went together to different yard good stores and shopped around for the material until everyone was satisfied. Jeanie of course, was my maid of honor and she wore a gown she designed and made herself of brushed satin, eggshell in color. I know Jeanie was heavy of heart that day, but she refused to show a hurtful countenance. Mama was now all a flutter. She sent out the invitations that Sam and I ordered. She ordered the Bridal Cake from the Cushman's Bakery in Parckhester instead of the one on Third Ave, stating, "the cakes taste better from the Jewish neighborhood. She engaged three ladies from the church to help her with the preparation of the wedding reception. The wedding reception was held in Sam's sister's house, Dottie because our apartment could not hold too many quests. My bridesmaids were Cindy and Anita who lived on our block. One of the girls from our church circle and Sam's other sister Edith.

My wedding gown was simple but exquisite. The gown was white brocaded taffeta with a trailing train. Two flounces across the waistline with full puffed sleeves to the wrists. The entire skirt was covered with pearl hearts Mama had tediously sewn on herself. We went together to a little Bridal shop in Brooklyn which Uncle Robert had advised us of. Mama said she didn't know that her little girl was so tiny. The gown was a size nine and it had to be altered to fit my tiny waistline. My headpiece was a gift from cousin May who worked in a hat shop in the City. Mama was beautifully dressed in a baby blue and beige lace gown. She had her hair dressed in the beauty parlor for the occasion. But I don't think she enjoyed how attractive she was that day; she had to bounce around so much making sure everything was under control.

I was dressed and ready before my bridesmaids. My Bermudian cousins, Endera and Mary had arrived two days before to give Mama a hand. Such an event, I thought to myself as I sat perched on Mama's Steamer trunk directly in front of her full-length mirror. Everyone is darting in and out of these two bedrooms getting dressed, and calling out to each other for assistance; and here I am all ready and waiting for the curtain to rise on the first act of the biggest event thus far in my life.

Daddy had long been ready. He stood tall and Regal in his Tuxedo eyeing me closely. I knew then that he was proud of his daughter although the words were not spoken. The photographer had arrived, and now the people in the building and neighborhood had gathered outside our front door, to see me come down the steps on the arm of my father.

But one thing I must surely mention and never will I ever forget, is what transpired with my father and I before I left my parents home to become the new Mrs.

Green. Everyone had left the apartment and was down the steps in a flurry of excitement. Daddy hesitated, and whispered quietly, "Lets kneel right here and say a little prayer before we leave." We both knelt down at the old upholstered chair in the corner, and Daddy spoke a few sentences almost inaudibly. He was asking the Lord to bless his daughter before she left the home of her girlhood. Such a quiet unobtrusive person but a giant of a man in the sight of God and in the eyes of his daughter.

Our wedding vows were spoken in the beautiful Victory Baptist Church on Union Ave in the Bronx, with about one hundred of our friends and relatives together. We honeymooned in Niagara Falls and Crystal Beach for two weeks. We visited some of Sam's old buddies in Upstate New York. We took loads of pictures, and we eagerly anticipated opening the door that was ajar to our new found love life and marriage.

Muriel Ratteray Green

CHAPTER NINE

The Journey

When going on a trip the smart traveler usually prepares himself for the journey. Plans are made and considerations for the climate and environment are taken into account. Luggage is packed tightly and neatly with clothes and toiletry, and a first aide kit is a necessary item. Marriage is a journey, and we the marriage partners are the sojourners; who embark on this trip as unprepared as the fledglings who are pushed out of their nests at the dawning of springtime.

We thought ourselves smart and chic travelers. We had good beginnings and all the needed equipment as we thought needed to make this run a fruitful and meaningful one. But as most folks know and understand some things cannot be learned from books. Birds cannot learn to fly without trying out their wings and you cannot learn to bake a cake without working with the ingredients.

Sam and I shared a large five-room apartment on the second floor on Home Street and Jackson Ave with his mother. The room had deep windows overlooking the Campus of Morris High School. Our apartment house stood at the top of the Home Street Hill. This was a beautiful area at the time with tree-lined streets and the famous Boston Road just one short block over.

Although dear Mother had all her belongings with us she didn't always stay with us. She enjoyed traveling back and forth from Staten Island to the Bronx visiting her grandchildren. She had her bedroom at the end of a long hallway. The north end of the hallway opened into two bedrooms and the large living room on the right. A big kitchen next to the bathroom also opened off from the hallway. As I look back now in recall, that kitchen was the main room and most important in the whole apartment. It had a large top to bottom window with a fire escape. We had lots of space for a large table and chairs and a huge refrigerator. We had a large Double Decker stove and oven with the black letters "Slattery" printed on the doors of the oven. A white enamel sink and washtub was in one corner, and a pulled down laundry dryer hung over head of the sink. I had never seen such an arrangement before in an apartment, but later it proved beneficial with all the dozens of diapers that had to be dried there in the kitchen, near the warm cozy stove. A deep wood old time cupboard stood behind the kitchen door, but there one fascination to me was the alcove over the kitchen table with four open shelves, the top shelf being curved where anything desired could be on display. Here's where I placed some of my wedding gifts and changed the display from time to time as I so wished according to the time of the year or the season.

I fell in love with the small bedroom between the living room and ours. At the time Sam and I moved into the apartment, it was full of the left over discarded things from Sam's absconded family. As they grew up and left their mother's home, they each left forgotten stuff behind. But all this was dispersed of in a matter of a few weeks, and before any infants arrived. I called this room the nursery. There was a "Rag Man," with his horse and outdated dilapidated wagon which passed through Home Street every Monday morning, tinkling his bells at the top of the hill, calling out "Rags 5 cents a lb." He'd watch and wait a few minutes while shades went up and heads peeped out to see who was selling their rags for extra change. Thus we cleaned out that little extra room we used for our babies over a period of nine years.

Sam had a healthy appetite and he loved to eat. This I discovered from the time of the picnic episode. Mama always wanted to show me the basics in the kitchen. But it was always Jeanie who wanted to learn the culinary arts. I knew neither how to make porridge or peel potatoes at the time of my marriage. But much in love with my new husband and eager to please, I soon learned. Sam never complained. He ate everything I cooked for him and all was by trial and error. His sisters and dear mother gave me a few pointers and I soon learned to make good hot wholesome meals. By the end of our first year of marriage I was able to cook and serve an impressive meal for us and invited company. Marriage was fun, we were very much engrossed in each other and as we both agreed we were still on our honeymoon.

We spent our first Anniversary in Washington D.C. This was the first time I had been this far south in our country. I had heard the word segregation often time enough. Had read about and heard our Preachers here in the North preach against segregation. I knew that our Negro population in the North were not treated equally when it came to jobs, housing, education. These conditions were tolerated thus far and swept under the covering of suspicion and fear. I personally had never encountered any adverse attitudes towards myself because of my skin coloring, but I knew these attitudes did exist. I had read about it in the magazines and newspaper that dared to attack the subject. But here down in Washington D.C. in a little Luncheonette; directly in sight of the Dome of the White House, symbol of freedom an justice we were told we could not be served at the tables. We ordered coffee and ham and cheese sandwiches for our breakfast, but we had to go around to the back door to pay for it and eat it. Sitting on the curb stones were the other patrons with colored skins and here too we sat to eat while the traffic raced by on the highway. I now knew firsthand what this was all about. I was made aware of what our fore fathers grew up with; had gone through, and how the burdens of ignorance and hatred on the part of the white population had stunted them as a people. The civil war had long been fought and won. The slaves had gained their freedom, but both races of people were wrapped up in a bondage of fear and obscurity. I realized now that it would take a lot of energy in demonstration, prayer and faith to make true freedom of souls and bodies a reality.

During the second year of marriage, I discovered I was carrying my first baby. I was young strong and happy. I enjoyed an uneventful pregnancy. I visited my doctor in the Maternity Clinic of the Bronx Hospital, and the doctor was pleased with my well being and progress. My first boy a healthy seven and a half pound, round pink human being entered this planet on June 22, 1950 at 7 AM on a Thursday morning. We thought, Sam and I no child in the world was as beautiful as ours. He is squalls were loud and strong. He seemed to be saying. "I am here, I am here!" "I arrived take notice of me." "I will never let you forget my presence." His fists were ready and beating the air, and his little pink feet could be heard kicking and thumping in his bassinet before he was months old. And so it was this precious matrix arrived on the scene, and no prouder father in all the world was his Daddy, and he was named for him. I knew then, as a young woman that my baby boy was sent from God, and that he would be called by God as his name Samuel denotes.

The nurses attending me in the hospital come to me in the afternoon of the same day of his birth and told me, I must try to get out of bed and walk. It was a new procedure to get the women up and moving earlier as opposed to keeping them in bed for a week. As I sat in the chair next to my bed, I rocked my new baby in his cozy blue blanket. My radio was on with strains of soft evening music filling the room with sweet quietness. The program was interrupted. I listened to the news, broadcasting a new turn of events. There were now impending clouds of war on the far East horizon. The Korean War had broken out on June 22, 1950, my son's date of birth. What impact these new turn of events would have upon my young son who had just made his debut in this vale of tears.

My new duties came to me easy. I seemed to be born to motherhood. Sam was a model husband and father. We were on our journey, the road was not bumpy and the signposts indicated no obstacles ahead. Of course Sammy Jr. had his crying sprees and his teething days, but in all he presented a healthy well nourished baby. But at the age of six months he became quite ill. We had taken him out of the bassinet and bought a beautiful wooden crib for him. His legs and arms were strong, and he could be heard thumping and cooing when awake. We both were light sleepers and were aware of his every movement at this early age. Our bedroom was large airy, and sunny, so Sammy Jr. and all his accouterments had occupied one side of our bedroom. We both heard his restless routing around in the crib one night and we jumped up to investigate. Sam grabbed his son up in a hurry, young Sammy was blue in color and unable to breathe. Sam blew breath into his nostrils and mouth while I called out to the Lord, as my mother had done so before me. After a few gasps Sammy had begun breathing again. But his chest was heavy with mucous and he certainly had trouble in breathing. We dressed the baby and ourselves hurriedly and took him to the Bronx Hospital where he was born. At the hospital, they diagnosed him as asthmatic and kept my baby to treat him. They placed him in an Oxygen Tent and hydrated him with medicated I.V. fluids. The journey now on the road of marriage was now showing some few variations. We were no longer a couple but a family with another human being who was totally dependant on us for their well being. What an awesome thought! Could we meet the challenge? Yes we would, just as our parents did before us we would meet the challenge with he help of the Lord.

Jeanie stuck close by us now, and she became almost our built in babysitter. Mama and daddy were both awestruck with their new grandchild and Mama was ready with all kinds of information and advice in baby care. One month before my second baby girl was born, Sammy made his second birthday. From the very first my doctor was not satisfied with this pregnancy. The doctor was concerned about my heart and placed me on a low sodium diet. He advised me to curtail some of my household duties and to take naps in the afternoon with my feet elevated. I tried to follow his directions, but as I can recall I never felt any physical discomfort, therefore I did not take all his admonitions seriously.

I was sleeping peaceful one night when I was awakened by a very soft voice, whether the voice was within me or not, at this time, I do not know, but I did experience a calming spirit that seemed to envelope me. I got up quickly and sat on the edge of my bed. The voice, whether within me or outside of me was whispering so convincingly? **Her Name Is Valerie Dianne.** I don't remember writing the name down, or waking Sam to tell him of this experience. But I do know that in the morning when I first gazed into my dresser mirror, I saw in my own handwriting the name Valerie Dianne written on a piece of paper an stuck in the corner of the mirror.

After one of my routine visits to the maternity clinic the doctor convinced me to take a short stay in the hospital for bed rest, to monitor my diet, and to insure a safe delivery. So dear Mother took over the care of baby Sammy with the help of Jeanie and Jesus.

All the preparations from then on for my new baby were in pink. The small bedroom between ours and the living room was freshly painted in an old rose pink and we added pink and white curtains for this was to be my little girl's room.

Sammy had now already taken over half of our bedroom with his crib and toys. He was becoming a healthy boy, bright as a button, and with a brilliant talent for memorization at such an early age. He remembered songs and Nursery Rhymes at the first hearing and enjoyed clapping and singing for whoever would audience him. He was able to recite the 23rd Psalm when he was a little more than two years old and did so at our Christmas Dinner Party, jumping up and down on his Grandmother Green's lap with little prompting from his Daddy.

As I stated before my doctor was very apprehensive about my health. I had a heart murmur and elevated blood pressure I was not in any pain or discomfort but I welcome the fact that I could play Lady of Leisure at least for a short period of time before my added duties of baby care and household responsibilities were upon me. And so I rested in the fact that my God was in control, that he knew all about my body, and that he was going to bring me and my baby through to a safe delivery. But the stay was longer than two weeks. The Doctor in charge did not want to let me go home for fear I would overdo, and so I spent "Mother's day" that year away from my little family. Sam was a very kind and loving husband and he came visiting, bearing gifts of flowers and stuffed animals for the occasion.

When Valerie Dianne was ready she made her regal entrance into the world. She was a beautiful pink girl with a radiant smile and two big blue gray saucer shaped eyes. A perfect cherub she was, how awesome and precious. She cried on cue, but not demanding with robust quells as presented by her brother. I snuggled her close to my heart and whispered in her black curly mob of hair. "God has named you already and before you were born He knew all about you." "Truly my sweet, you have been sent from the Lord." After the birth of Valerie the Doctor at the maternity clinic advised me not to have any more children, and we thought ourselves to be the perfect American family of four.

After a few months of lazing around the house thanks to the help of Dear Mother (Sam's Mother) and Jeanie I was able to just rest and enjoy my babies. Valerie gained and thrived according to the baby charts and was an easy baby to manage. Soon her cooing and gurgling could be heard through out the house. Sammy became quite curious. I don't think he could imagine himself ever in such a helpless and dependant state as his baby sister. He asked numerous questions. His little fists were always tight with crayons or one of his small trucks. He watched with special interest every morning while I bathed and dressed her. He examined her tiny hands and feet, and had to have her warm bottles tested on the back of his hands before I gave them to Valerie. Surely as he insisted he was "helping" Mommy with the baby. One day I accidentally left a safety pin, open and stuck on the inside of her bassinet. Sammy was left in charge while stepped aside a short minute to get her bottles. In a swift second Valerie let out a loud shriek, I looked back at my baby; one of her little feet were bleeding. Sammy wanted to know what would happen if he stuck a pin in her feet. Well that started the lessons that I had to teach them all their lives; that they must not hurt each other; and that Valerie was the baby now as he is the big strong brother with the responsibility of looking out for those helpless and younger than himself. He looked up at me with his big inquisitive eyes. "Didn't mean to hurt baby sister," he said. I only wanted to play. When Valerie gets older she'll be your playmate, I kissed his pink cheeks, and Mommy should not have left pins so close to baby. I smacked my own hands, called myself naughty Mommy, and told Sammy he must always help me to remember to be careful with the baby. The incident soon forgotten but the lesson was well learned. Sammy guarded and watched over his sister, for he was the big strong guy, next in line to his Daddy.

We often had dinner parties at home now even though I had the care of another baby. Valerie fit well in my schedule, she was happy and healthy as long as she was bathed, fed and burped. I now began to experiment in the kitchen with different dishes. Edith and Dottie, Sam's sisters were always willing to show me a new cooking secret. Mama and Daddy were still living on 167th Street off Prospect Ave. Mama seemed very pensive and remote at times. She and Jeanie always came to my Thursday night dinner, but Mama appeared quiet and subdued now. This was out-of character for Mama, she always had something to say, a story to tell even though something had been told over and over again. Mama was always dressed carefully for these occasions and Jeanie was always there with her camera. Daddy rarely showed up. He preferred to stay at home and keep company with his books, in his favorite old upholstered chair in the corner of the living room. On occasion he would visit us for Christmas or Thanksgiving, leaving gifts for Sammy and Valerie half hidden behind the others under the decorated Christmas tree. Mama wore decorated combs in her now web like white hair and she sat straight and erect at her daughter and son-in-law's table. There was always at least ten at the Christmas table, beautifully decorated by Sam himself that he enjoyed doing so much. We loved to display our wedding gifts, and if it were the Christmas season, the tree would be blinking with its multi-colored lights and ornaments.

But I must get back to Mama. Something about her spirit perturbed me. She seemed resigned and doleful and hesitant in fully joining in with the good natured laughter around the table.

When I spoke to Sam, what I felt, after our quests had gone home, he seemed bewildered and did not know how to answer me. Did he see what I saw? Feel what I felt? A woman just in her early fifties with a broken spirit. What was happening to her? Was she allowing the natural course of menopause diminish her usual jovial attitude? Or was their some other unknown unspoken areas of her inner being, being ravished by forces she herself could not identify. I know now that if Mama were still alive in this era of time, we would have a label for her troubles and we would call it the Empty Nest Syndrome. Looking back now I know that's what my Mama was suffering from. She had not one who literally needed her busy serviceable hands and ready advice, as she thought. My Mother-in-Law, Dear Mother as we called her was always ready to baby sit when needed, and Jeanie came almost every day to help care for the babies so I wouldn't overtire. Now Jeanie was always going or coming. Always keeping her busy, busy as I presumed, trying to bind up the wounds of her broken heart. Daddy and Mama did not seem to communicate verbally and if so only to transpire the business of keeping their home together. It was clear that Mama was suffering inside. Did she feel sorrow for her oldest daughter Jeanie, who clearly had given her heart to Ronald, even though he could not accept it? Did she feel any animosity towards her Mimsie who had turned all energies and love into caring for her family? Had I failed my own dear mother I wondered. I loved her dearly and tried to show it in different ways and endearments. But she was content to sit at home and peer out from behind her curtains and feel the emptiness in her heart and breast. This was becoming clear to me slowly and surely as the dawn breaks through the gray skies. In Mama's unspoken reasoning, it appeared to me, she had lost her two daughters, surely as if someone had snatched them out of her arms.

Jeanie was lost to Ronald and her dreams of what might have been, and Mimsie was won over by Sam, the young man who only sought companionship from her youngest daughter.

Soon Mama began complaining of headaches and weakness. She would not visit a doctor. Daddy sat at the foot of her bed, and gazed on her. It was clear now after a few weeks of her illness that he was becoming concerned. Jeanie stayed closer to home now. She cooked and cleaned for Daddy and Mama and had meals ready for Daddy when he got home from the Grand Central at 6 P.M. But Mama did not revive at this time. She became restless and stayed in bed days on end. When I came to see her and brought little Sammy to see her, her eyes would lighten up, but her face had lost its roundness. Still she refused to have a Doctor look at her, stating, "I'll be alright in a few more days." Sometimes Mama was bright and would look out the window and water her plants but these days were becoming few and far between.

One Sunday morning I was sitting in Church with little Sammy snuggled up next to me when one of the ushers tapped me on the shoulder. He said in a whispered voice, "Sister Muriel, your dad's outside, he wants to speak with you now." A shudder ran down my back, something's happened to Mama I thought. I gathered Sammy and myself and went outside. Daddy was parked outside in his old 1942 Ford. He looked up at me; his lips were drawn and tight.

He said in a dry emotionless voice. "I hate to have to tell you this;" He licked his lips his brow was furrowing now. "Your mother left the house this morning in her bedroom clothes and was wandering around in the streets looking for help." "A lady across the street recognized her and called us from the window." "Oh my Lord, help us" I exclaimed. "Where is Mama now?" I said getting into the front seat with little Sammy in the middle. "I could not leave her in this state of mind and she would not go back into the house with me." "She acted like she didn't know Jeanie and me; she was crying I need someone to help me, and Jeanie and I were right there." "The Ambulance came and got her Mimsie, they treated her very gently, they talked kindly to her, and Mama went with them just as quietly as if she were a little lamb.

Daddy's eyes were sad his face was thin and drawn. He had been under this burden so long. Mama not being her real self, and he did not know why. I saw a middle aged man, loving his wife and family, but broken and unable to cope and not knowing just how to bring together the torn and tangled threads in the Tapestry of his Life. I bowed my head, and thought I was going to cry. I thought to myself. How could I allow something like this to happen to my Mama? I loved her dearly. She had been the most important person to me before I met my husband. Daddy started the car and we drove away from the church towards his apartment. "Don't worry Daddy, everything is going to be alright." I knew I had to be strong for him and Jeanie now. I knew that Jeanie was suffering silently in her own private hell. It was clear that she could not convey her sadness to anyone not even to me even though I tried to show her I was there for her in so many ways. I could not break up now, the dam of tears would over-flow and engulf us all, and I had to be strong for Daddy now, he had no one else. I suddenly felt a mantle of peace fall over my shoulders. "God has been with us before" "He has brought us through quite a few events." "The depression days, the war years, Jeanie's sickness, and her loss of Ronald; for he was surely lost to her just as if he had been missing in action." "If he does not remove the problem, so the Holy Spirit within me was counseling, he will help us to get through it." Mama now in the Hospital will get the professional help she could not get at home. God give me the faith to believe I whispered to myself. Help me to believe. My spirit became calmer now. I do believe, I do, and after all I am child of the King.

Mama's first two weeks in the hospital was spent in Lincoln Hospital in the Bronx. Here she was very quiet and withdrawn and hardly spoke a word to anyone. Her new behavior was unreal to me. Her appetite was very poor. She hardly said anything to anyone, and she sat for hours with her hands motionless in her lap. The Doctors decided she needed further care and closer supervision, so she was sent to a sanitarium in upstate N.Y. Mama was given her own room and had kitchen privileges she shared with the other clients. This was hard for me to accept that mama was truly mentally and emotionally disturbed, but her Doctors stated that time and lots of TLC would bring her around.

Mama's sickness seemed to have an adverse affect on Jeanie. At times she seemed unable to cope with the fact that Mama was no longer in the home. She spent most of her time now helping me with little Sammy. She would return home in the afternoon to start supper for Daddy and serve him the meal. I watched after her one afternoon as she walked down Home Street Hill. How slow her steps and narrow her frame had become, only 26 years old now, and a whisper of a woman. Dear God I sighed, Dear

God. Mama did not make a speedy recovery. She needed constant care and vigilance. But I had not given up on Mama. My prayers became much stronger and I knew that God had a purpose in all life's events. I totally put my trust in him. Somehow I had sweet assurance that come what may the Lord was going to make thing right. My whole life and times were in his hands.

Jeanie stuck by us closely now. I knew that by 9 o'clock in the morning she would be coming up Home Street Hill to be with me and my babies. Soon after Daddy would leave for his job at the Grand Central Station, she would do her early morning chores and start out to our house. She loved little Sammy especially; she would play with him and sing little crony songs to him. But the real robust Jeanie was slowly pining away right before my eyes. This was evident to me when one Saturday morning she came to visit, I noticed how gaunt and pale her cheeks had become, and how breathless she was from climbing the two flights of steps to our apartment. I chided with her for coming. She said she was lonely without Mama in the house. But she soon took my advice and stayed closer to home avoiding the hill and the steps which was against her. Nonetheless Jeanie became very weak in the days following and had to go to the Hospital for treatments. The Doctors at the hospital said her heart was under a strain. Her heart was not able to pump normally enough blood to the rest of her body. Her stay in the Hospital was short lived.

Jeanie went to be with Jesus on Nov 6, 1952 at 6 P.M. in the evening just as sweetly and quietly as she had lived her young life. My dear sweet Jeanie had left my side and this world of sorrows. I was overwhelmed. I thought that I would not be able to contain my heart that felt crushed in my chest. Sam's sisters came and rocked me in their arms. Sam stood by to steady and comfort me. My church family prayed for me and sustained me. But Daddy had no one real person that he could rely on at this time, but somehow he proved to be a bulwark of strength he said came from God. The next problem was how to tell Mama, that now she had truly lost Jeanie.

We had a quiet funeral with family and friends and surprisingly it was not very sad. Many of her favorite hymns were sung and we consoled ourselves in the fact that we would meet Jeanie again in heaven someday.

I sat between Daddy and Sam on the front pew of our little church that had now moved further up in the Bronx. I watched intently the mourners go by to view Jeanie's still form in her casket. She was dressed all in white and looked like and Indian princess. Her face was not sad but peaceful. I looked again and there before my very eyes stood the form of a waif of a young man, dressed in a dark pin striped suit.

His wavy black hair glistening in the dimly lit room. The people in line waiting to view the body moved away from him. He put out his hand and touched her cheek. He bent down to kiss her and I heard him whisper but audibly. "My Glamour Girl Jeanie." Daddy's arm became rigid under mine. I pressed him back in his seat. Sam's knee pressed hard against mine. Ronald was saying his last goodbyes. I became peaceful in my soul, for I knew for sure he could never ever hurt her again for she was now resting in the arms of Jesus.

The next hurdle that we had to get over was how to tell Mama about Jeanie's death. We spoke to her Doctors about it and they advised us to tell her so and they would be on standby with medication and counseling in case she overreacted.

Mama did not overreact. She looked at the both of us and quietly stated. "I knew this was going to happen a long time ago." "How long can we live with a broken heart?" she asked. She took out a little snapshot of Jeanie she had with her when Jeanie was just a teenager and showed it to us. "This is the way I see her in my dreams she said" "This is my real Jeanie."

We looked at each other, Dad and I; the realization had broken through. Mama was conversing with us. Saying sentences that had meaning. I suddenly understood now. Mama knew that her eldest daughter was not able to hold up under the pressures of life. She saw her daughter sadden with a broken heart; and she was compelled to watch the scene, helpless from day to day. This weakened Mama's own spirit and she herself was unable to cope with these feelings. Mama began to recuperate slowly now. Her appetite picked up and she was beginning to participate in the new rehab programs they set-up for her. This was a bright new ray of hope for me, and even though we were advised it would take some time before she would fully recover, we knew that she had started in that direction.

Sam was now working long hours in a plant on Long Island to keep his little American family of four warm and well fed. We were now living in the mid 1950's. As I recall the 1950's were called the "Fabulous Fifties." I now had a telephone and a black and white television set, one of the first of its kind in our circle of friends and relatives. The picture was some times snowy and fuzzy, but you only had to learn the art of manipulating the knobs, and soon the picture would come in clearer.

In the early days, the television set was a great boon for young mothers with active growing children. Howdy Doowdy became the #1 baby sitter for most preschoolers, and Ed Sullivan took over a large slot of entertainment hours on Sunday nights at 8PM.

My little family was healthy and well now and soon I discovered there was to be another addition to our family. I was becoming an old hen at this birthing game. My days were now filled with more planning. I planned neither for boy or girl but for a new baby. I was neither elated nor frustrated at the thought of a new little life growing inside of me. There was plenty of room now in our apartment. Dear Mother had left her bedroom to us and had started on a round of visits to her children which ended in a permanent arrangement with her daughter Edith. We certainly had plenty of baby clothes and baby furniture and one more would make us richer. I had an easy pregnancy and did not grow very large. The doctors had advised me "Not to," but my God was looking down and smiling on my little family.

I sometimes sorrowed for Jeanie, and looked often at her pictures. I often felt her spirit near me, and Sam and I often spoke about her. Her name was never avoided in our day to day living. We kept her picture on our fireplace mantle, and Sammy and baby Valerie knew at an early age who Auntie Jeanie was.

What a perfect little family we had. Sammy Jr. as bright as a button, with his little spider songs and Valerie, my pink doll baby as I called her, who always had a ready smile from ear to ear, no matter what time of day or night she was awakened. I was up early every morning to start my daily duties. I never stayed in bed past 6 A.M. Sam's breakfast had to be made, his lunch packed and off he would go to catch his ride that would take him to his new job on Long Island. Then my round of duties would begin. Where does a mother love begin and end? It is like a never ending circle going round and round again. My children filled my days. I sometimes worried about Mama in an Upstate Hospital waiting for visitors or mail. I went to see her as often as I could I went with some of my church circle of friends with our Rev. Ellison and his wife. Sometimes she was happy to see us and sometimes she seemed glad and relieved when we left. I believe Mama was becoming "Sacked In" into her new surroundings. But I had a strong determination within myself that Mama was going to get well. No matter how long it would take I was willing to go to any lengths and make any sacrifice so that Mama could live a normal life in an outside society.

My second son Victor David arrived on a Holiday, Nov 11th 1953 Armistice Day on another Thursday as did the others at 8 A.M. What a surprise baby he was. He was perky and spirited! His insistent angry cries seemed to be saying, what am I doing out here in this unfriendly world. I knew my new boy was born with talent and that he was going to erase all the dark clouds on his horizon with a quick stroke of his magic paintbrush. There was only seventeen months between Victor David and

Valerie. Now Sammy Jr. was the senior sibling. He learned his new role as big brother to Valerie and baby Vicky soon and learned it well.

Soon after this event Glen Bernard put in his appearance. He was in a big hurry. He just could not wait out his appointed nine months time. Eight months was long enough for him to be separated from his ready made family. He had only traces of fingernails, no eyebrows and big brown eyes, ready to play jokes on who ever notice him. His Daddy named him Glen Bernard after a football player whose picture appeared on the front page of the Daily News on the morning he was born. He was just like his name Glen denotes. A bubbly well of joy ready to move into your heart and take possession.

Now Valerie was the little lady in the group. I truly was happy and contented with my little family now. Four children in five years was quite a feat for me and sometimes a strain on the purse strings. But thank God, He did provide for us. We never missed a meal, and we had each other to keep us happy and on our toes as the days came and went. We both, Sam and I decided it was time to call a halt to family making. So I channeled all my energies into training and shaping the lives of my four little ones. This was a twenty-four hour a day job, a task not to be taken lightly with short cuts. I was well on my journey. It was not just a marriage picnic, but also a family trip. I saw that the trip would be a long winding road. Sometimes tedious and bumpy along the way. The Lord was with me, for I felt his presence and divine guidance every step of the way. I confided these feelings to Sam. He made no agreeable remarks to these feelings. Was his thinking different from mine? We both had the same religious upbringing. This was one of the factors that brought us together. Why was he so hesitant now to join me in the spiritual upbringing of our children? Or maybe I was simply mistaken in this new observation; surely I certainly hoped that I was.

Muriel Ratteray Green

CHAPTER TEN

The Trip Continues

Where does the strength come from when one is confronted with a need? A need for strong arms, longer days, quiet hours and more understanding, mercifully the need might not even be recognized, but that does not cancel it out. There are twenty four hours in a day. I tried to take advantage of each waking hour. To waste time was like throwing away money. I could not just sit still for fifteen minutes or half an hour and just relax, my mind was working ahead of my energies. There were so many things needed to be done at one time. My own two arms, hands and feet, no matter how swift in motion were not enough to attack and finish all the tasks of the day that routinely presented themselves. I soon realized that there were other arms, stretching out, helping and upholding me. They were the arms of God. When I finally, went to sleep at night, if only for a few short hours, the sleep was so deep and merciful that when I awoke, I truly was refreshed and ready to start all over again. This is the way I always felt, like a race horse in those early days of my journey into marriage and motherhood. I felt there was nothing too hard for my undertaking. Nothing too strenuous to pull or drag, and nothing too hurtful or heartrending that I could not shrug off or forget. Thus I engrossed myself in my daily round of chores of raising my four little ones and closed my eyes to all the signposts along the way. I asked myself many times where does all this manpower come from? I will tell you now in words plain and simple; my help came from the Lord. The Lord God Almighty, The Creator of the Universe in the person of Jesus Christ. If he had not been my abiding, counselor and friend, I might not have made it on this part of my journey. But as I mentioned earlier in my story, I recognized earlier in life that I was of Royal Blood that God was my Heavenly Father and I was a Child of the King. I felt a comforting sense of security that as the songwriter wrote some years back. "His eye is on the Sparrow and I know He watches me."

In the very early days when the little ones were very young, I never left them alone. Sam's mother who we called dear Mother would come by for a couple weeks stay and give me a hand with them. Then she would announce time for her to check the others out and off she would go with her packed suitcase and a jar of her famous turkey soup. She always gave me encouragement and told me to be happy and proud that I had my whole family at such an early age of twenty seven. Sometimes they were really very sick with colds and fevers, the chicken pox and the measles. At one time I do remember having the four of them sick at one time. Sam would be very interested and he helped me all he could. Sometimes we had to take them to the Bronx Hospital Emergency Room when I couldn't bring down a high temperature after repeated alcohol sponge baths. The episodes usually passed after two or three days at a time. But the more worrisome days were when Sammy Jr. and Glen had asthmatic attacks. It was very frightening to see them trying to get air into their lungs. We had to be very careful of their diet and their environment. Certain things they could not eat; chicken, rice, chocolate, peanuts were excluded from their diets. We could not have any furry pets or birds. No rugs on the floors and dust had to be kept at a minimum. Thus we cooperated with the doctors for the good of Sammy and Glenny, but still they suffered many harsh and vicious attacks of wheezing and coughing and had to be hospitalized on many occasions.

But there was an undercurrent of faith and love sustaining me, and blessed assurance that the Lord was going to see me through these trying days. I wrote to Oral Roberts the T.V. Healing Evangelist and asked him to pray for Sammy Jr. especially who at the time was the sickest. He did just that and sent me back a hand signed letter, with two little swatches of prayer cloths I eagerly pinned to Sammy's undershirts. In no time my eldest son started to gain weight and his cheeks became rosy and full again. He soon became a well built child, perfect in mind and body. I perceived that the hand of God was on him. There was five years between Sammy and Glenny, and Valerie and Vicky's birthday fit in between those five years. When Glen turned three years old, it seemed it was his turn now to suffer the untold miseries of asthma. I was kept busy in the clinics with Glenny. His eyes would water, cough incessantly and his breath would come in short gasps. He would say to me often, pointing to his chest. "The Wheezy Man Got Me Mommy!" He had to go to the Bronx Hospital for shots. At one time he was desensitized with as many as twelve little under-the-skin pricks with the substance that was suspected to cause the asthma. If the little skin pricks turned into cartwheels then that substance was the culprit that caused his illness. The tests proved fruitful. The Doctors determined that he was allergic to chicken, rice, nuts and chocolate.

When I told Glen that he could no longer eat chicken and nuts, rice and chocolate he was very sad. "Oh no! he said, "I'll just have to get prayed for and be healed like Sammy." My heart leaped for joy. What beautiful child like faith. But at this time I did not write any faith healer or evangelist. But I started to pray earnestly for Glen, and especially for his healing. And I prayed earnestly for each one separately, for I knew they were individuals and each had their own special needs. But most of all they needed to know the Savior in the pardoning of their sins. They needed to know this for themselves. My experience with Jesus Christ could not help them.

I could no longer attend my Bronx Church, because now our family had made several moves. From the Apt on Home Street we moved to the Apartment on Brook Ave in the Bronx, which became very distasteful. The rooms in these Bronx Project Apartments were beautiful but the environment was unsatisfactory for rearing children. Sam had the good foresight to see the environment for what it was, and he moved his little family again to Queens in a very nice Project Complex, and here the children began to grow and flourish to our happy amazement. They were bussed out to different schools, especially Victor and Valerie who in the second and third grades attended the same school.

We also discovered that we were in walking distance to Bethel Gospel Tabernacle, a beautiful, faith believing Pentecostal church with a forceful dynamic Pastor. The children and I began attending Sunday morning service as regularly as my strength and endurance would allow. Sometimes the children rebelled against the preparations of dressing up and wearing Sunday best. They preferred rather to run about in sneakers and jeans and play in the playgrounds that the projects had provide for the children. But I taught them early on, that Sunday was the "Lords Day," and even if we could not get to church to worship for some reason or other, that Sunday was to be treated with reverence and respect, and not a day for game playing and chasing about on the grounds. This they understood.

The landscape around these buildings were beautiful, spacious, clean and well kept. The children were safe. I could look out my wide kitchen window, and watch them at least a blocks' distance away. One day while getting the children ready for church, little Glenny said to me. "Mommy let the Minister pray for me so the Wheezy Man will go away. I made no direct answer to him at the time, but I knew I had in mind what I wanted to do. I wanted to be sure that little Glen was ready and receptive. That same Sunday I brought Glenny up on the Pulpit at the end of the service and three ministers laid their hands on Glen, anointed him with oil and prayed the prayer of faith for his asthmatic condition to leave him. He showed marked improvement from that day on. Soon Glen was eating chicken and rice and nut chocolate candy along with his siblings. I was so grateful and made aware of the power of God. Only a little grain of faith, the size of a mustard seed was needed for God to work a healing miracle in Glen's little body. I watched him carefully, I was not skeptical, but I id not want to give the adversary a chance to invade and dissuade my child's faith. Hence with the Lords help and healing hands over our little group, we kept afloat the sea of life. Yes sometimes the journey takes you over bumpy roads, restless seas and mountains hard to climb.

Now the children and I had found a place to worship where we could attend regularly and in walking distance from our Queens Apartment. They were thriving each of them and doing well in school.

At this time I was able to visit Mama quite frequently, and on occasion I found her to be quite perky. I say on occasion because she had her down side days. There were days when she would sit very quietly and not communicate to anyone. She was never irate or violent in behavior only pensive and morose. But I knew that prayer and supplication on her behalf would bring her around. Sam made provisions for me to visit her, and when I did I always brought her goodies, crackers, cookies and cheese and lots of reading materials, for Mama loved to read. One day Mama said outright, "When am I going home?" Oh! this was what I was longing to hear. I knew now that she understood that that place was not her home and she did not belong there permanently. I talked it over with Sam when I got home and we agreed that Mama could stay with us, where she would be cared for and watched closely if it was agreeable with Daddy.

In the mean time Dear Mother's health began to wane. Her heart had become weakened, and so she had to remain in bed most of the time with her daughters in attendance on her. Something odd, but natural was taking place here. Some called it The Full Circle, some call it the revolving door, and I call it a human phenomenon. It's the reversal of rolls. When children once dependant on their parents, become parents to their parents. This has always been but not so noticeable as at the present, because folks were not living past their late middle years as they are doing at the present time. It soon became evident to me, that this was mama's gut feeling. That she no longer was useful and that if she lived long enough she would become dependent on her daughter, and that I would have to care for her as I did my little ones. Mama did not realize that caring for her would be one of my greatest pleasures. I could never ever repay Mama for all that she taught me in my early days, and how she introduced me to the true Christian way of life. Nonetheless mama continued to show improvement. She was allowed to come home on weekend passes. The children were elated and they with their noise and childish play did not prove to be too much for her. At last the doctors were satisfied with her improvement and they allowed Mama to come home to stay. We had plenty of space, for if there's room in the heart, there's room in the home. The boy's room was large enough for them and their toys. Little Valerie was proud to share her bedroom with her Grand mommy. This worked out beautifully and the little ones were excited to have an extra Mommy in the home. "I'm going to try my hardest to spoil them," she said one evening sitting on the couch with little Glen perched happily on her lap. "Isn't that what Grandparents are supposed to do?" she added. I knew now that Mama had found her second home.

Daddy was still living in his old Bronx Apartment and he came out to Queens now and then to visit Mama. They both seemed satisfied with this arrangement. Sam was happy for me, and contented that my mind was at rest. It did not appear that Mama needed any careful watching and she adjusted easily to our family routine. She got up early every morning before Sam and I, made her toiletry, was fully dressed and as she called it, "waiting for whatever the day brings." She always wore an apron over her navy blue skirt with a hankie pinned to her waistband. Mama was now her old self again.

Time was fleeting by now. Sam was growing paunchy around the middle and losing some sprigs from his pate. I was beginning to get a little heavy around the middle also and some white strands were beginning to show up around my ears. But we were happy healthy and well. God had surely smiled on us. The children easily made friends with the neighbor's children and each one had their own little special buddy who they enjoyed playing with exclusively. We were now parents of Adolescents. Sammy at fourteen was shooting up tall and straight. He was reading everything and very much interested in Science. His father bought him a trumpet for his thirteenth birthday, and he had been taking trumpet lessons ever since. Valerie was a strong willed tomboy of a lady. She knew how to be kind and gentle with her Mommy and Grand mommy, but could hold her own in strength and stamina with her brothers. When I needed something hammered, fixed or put back in place, it was always Valerie who came to my rescue. But I also saw the beautiful blossom of femininity under that boyish veneer.

Vicky was my wanderer. Being a middle child it must have been difficult for him. He was always able to amuse himself, and when his surroundings became too boring or humdrum he would look for other adventures. He was a loving child, and I loved him dearly but he was not particularly attracted to anyone or anything. I always had to keep a special eye on Vicky when shopping in a store. He didn't seem to mind leaving me and wandering out the store and down the street looking for something new and different. Vicky was and still is an artist. Vicky, at an early age could interpret on paper anything that he saw or felt in a matter of minutes.

There was five years between Sammy and Glenny. As you recall I had four children in five years. Glenny was beginning to hold his own even though he was the baby in the family. To him everything was a great big joke, and he enjoyed so much playing pranks on others. He always had a riddle to tell and at a very early age he would keep his audience spellbound as he unraveled his tales of magic and mystery. How very different they were from each other, and how very much the same they were when I heard their prayers and kissed them good night and turned down the light. I would whisper to the Lord as I tiptoed away from their beds. God please keep them children forever." I knew this was a selfish wish but I only wanted to cherish their innocence.

Mama was like a ripening tomato on the vine. She had gained weight and her peachy color had returned to her cheeks. She was helping with the housework and the children's homework. She met and made new friends in our building complex. I knew that when Mama made fiends she was truly on the way to recovery. She now had a permanent babysitting job for a little boy in our building. She sometimes spent the night with them when his parents went out for the evening. This gave her a change of scenery and also a little extra spending change. She enjoyed taking bus rides and catching the sales in the new shopping malls in Queens. It appeared to me that everything was happening so fast and I could not keep up with anything. Were we being pushed into the fast lane of life? The shapes and shades of colors of the cars were changing from year to year. Ladies hemlines were dancing up and down from one season to the next. One year my feet were comfortable in baby doll shoes, and the next year, the pointed toes and spikes heels were in vogue. The beautiful love ballads, sung by Lena Horn, Diana Shore, Judy Garland and Frank Sinatra gave way to the crashing drum beats and guitar plunking of the Monkeys, or the Beatles, or whatever they chose to call themselves. The colored people, who emerged with "Negroes", were now calling themselves "I'm black and I'm proud." This called for a lot of soul searching on my part. I was not a particularly outspoken or opinionated person. But I did have inward pride, I was proud of my upbringing. I was proud of my husband Sam, who worked hard to keep his family together, and his wife did not have to go out to work to supplement his earnings. I was pleased and proud that Mama had snapped back into society after being shut away for so long from those she loved. But this was some new kind of pride that I saw and heard and read about in the newspapers.

These newcomers, The Black Panthers, they called themselves, marched into our church on New York Blvd in Queens one Sunday morning and filled up thirty seats. They were quiet and mannerly, wearing their black leather jackets and large wooly Afros. Were they in rebellion against the society that had ill-treated them and their forefathers or were they making a statement. I concluded they were doing both. New activists groups were cropping up everywhere. People were marching, carrying banners and flags expressing their sentiments. Sam was becoming involved. He joined political groups and campaigns and I watched and wondered from the sidelines. Sam rode down on a bus to Washington to see and hear Dr. Martin Luther King speak. I was truly proud of the Lady Rosa Parks who refused to ride in the back of a Southern Bus after working hard all day. I was proud of those stout hearted souls who sat at the lunch counters and refused to leave when harassed and their very lives threatened. I read the newspapers and I watched T.V. and prayed fervently. "Dear God, Help us, our Country is in a turmoil. The internal problems in our country that was squelched for so long were coming to the fore-front. There were better job opportunities for the black man, desegregation of schools not just on the books but also in actuality and voter registration in the southern states. These were the problems of the day and times. Dr. Martin Luther King Jr., Medgar Evers, along with others were our champions. They marched, they assembled, they sang and they prayed, endeavoring to use their mighty sling shots aimed at the forehead of that ugly giant called Bigotry. "Did they manage to fell him?" I think not. That old Giant called Bigotry is still hanging around under different names and guises using others ruses. But I am confident that with the help of the Lord and the new found strength and confidence of the young emerging black race, he will be struck down and we shall surely overcome some day.

Jack Kennedy was in the White House at the time of the civil right's movement in the U.S. in 1962. His brother Bobby appeared to be the Presidents' right hand man. Many crisis and state of the Union Problems were argued over and resolved between the two of them in the oval office. Jack Kennedy was in a reckless dangerous plight not only with political system of this country, but also with the dealings of the outside world. He visited the Berlin Wall and his "Ich Bin Ein Berliner" speech endeared him to the German People and to his countrymen at home. And there was always the younger brother. But the world community was becoming ruthless and so the inevitable occurrence took place on Nov 22, 1963. The President John F. Kennedy was the first of our time to befall an assassin's bullet.

Sam rounded up our four children and the neighborhood children down to the center of the playground where the flagpole was. There Sammy Jr. dressed in his boys scouts uniform played taps on his trumpet for our fallen President while the flag was raised half mast. The nonviolent Dr. Martin Luther King was the next to be cut down in his struggle for Civil Rights, on April 4, 1968. In June of the same year Bobby Kennedy stopped another assassin's bullet and truly plunged the country into a nightmare of shadowy despair. And so the country was in a mourning state for a good many years. People were sad and teary eyed everywhere. Flags remained at half-mast and Correta King and her children along with the Kennedy Clan were symbols of strength and dignity. Who was behind those who perpetrated such heinous crimes? The media was full of dark stories and pictures. After the death of Jack Kennedy, the new President Lyndon Banes Johnson took over the helm of the Old Ship of State. Slowly and with quiet trepidation he tried to put the pieces of his country back together again. New Civil rights Laws were passed and backed up by the President and the government, but not without struggle and bloodshed. The T.V. screen now became a very important reporting media for the American people. Here depicted before their very eyes was the cruelty of one race against the other. Dogs and heavy hosing of waters were used on those who were only using their right to demonstrate against the inequalities and injustices that were perpetrated against them. The black folks were taking their first steps towards freedom. The march had begun. The journey was along ways ahead and the road would be treacherous and the eyes of the World were upon us.

CHAPTER ELEVEN

Signposts

The early part of the 1960's brought The Worlds' Fair to Flushing Meadows Park in Queens N.Y.C. This was a place of great interest, experimentation and knowledge. The children visited the Fair at least half a dozen times with each other and also with their school classes. These excursions were learning opportunities for the children in the neighborhood. You could start out early every morning and walk about visiting as many pavilions as you could get to see in one day; do this everyday, and in one week still have covered only a small territory of exhibitions. The fair grounds were a vast fabulous place, covering all parts of topics and information. It depicted mostly the progress of man from his earliest beginnings, his discoveries, inventions of the present time and what he hoped to achieve by the end of the century.

Mama was not able to attend any of these visits to the New York Worlds' Fair because she was always busy with her baby sitting jobs, but we promised to see that she could make a visit before the Fair closed.

Something new was always happening with the children now. Sammy was blowing his trumpet in the school band, and Vicky was no longer a dependant sibling but venturing out on his own. It seemed he had already found a niche for himself at such an early age. He was very talented artistically, could use well his brushes and charcoal, and was planning on studying art in High School and entering the art field in some capacity. He knew just what he wanted to do when he grew up early on. Valerie was blossoming in mind and body, and was herself, an appointed bulwark against sibling aggression. She thought always that she had to solve all problems and squabbling that occurred between them before it reached my ears. By the time when I appeared on the scene amidst a verbal confrontation they had already presented a united front. "Don't worry Mommy," they would say, "Valerie settled it." I always wanted to know what it was that Valerie had to settle. It usually started over some game they were playing or some project they were putting together. Or one of them had borrowed another's property, and had failed to return it to its rightful owner. They would pit their strength against each other. They called it rough housing, Sam called it wrestling. I thought it to be detrimental, and I said so, and did forbid all sorts of squirmishes between them. But children in the adolescent years do not listen and sometimes have to be taught a lesson.

They usually would start their "just having fun" times on early Saturday mornings when they were all home from school together. I would be busy with the laundry in the kitchen. The game of checkers or "Money Mad" would usually start the fracas, and under the hum of the extracting washing machine, I would hear the muffled bumps and thumps of legs and arms on the floor of the boys' room. I would tiptoe down the hall, open the door to the boy's room and there on the floor to my consternation would be melee of fists punching and shoving and angry faces to match. I would shout loudly. "Who started all this?" They slowly calmed down, and looked one to the other. We all did piped Valerie, with defined bite marks under her lips. Yeah we all started it came Vicky's retort from under Sammy's tight headlock. It seemed as though it was Glen and Sammy against Vicky and Valerie in some sort of confrontation of strength. "O.K.", I said. "I will finish it." They did not know what I had in mind to do I had repeatedly warned them, no physical fights ever between them. This was prohibited as long as I was alive in their presence. I explained to them on many occasions, that they were all cut from the same piece of cloth and four slices cut from one pie. I ran the cold water into a big pot, hurriedly threw some ice cubes in and tiptoed down the hall to the outside of the boy's room. The four of them were still on the floor now, trying to settle the dispute verbally. I hastily flung open the door and threw the whole pot of iced cold water over them, and whispered quietly between clenched teeth. You guys started it, now you guys mop it up. They jumped up startled, soaked, each of them from head to toe in stark reality. "Now dry up, clean up, and shut up, I demanded, else your Daddy will add to it when he comes home. I thought about this isolated incident, days later and wondered if this was the right approach to their bickering and constant squabbling amongst themselves. Was there another way I could have handled the situation? I had talked with them calmly on many occasions, I had punished them and promised them but these tactics did not seem to work with my children. I did not want them at each other's throats all the time. I wanted them to love and respect each other as Jean and I so did. Sometimes it worried me that young children in a close knit loving family could be so aggressive towards each other even in the innocence of a quiet game. Nonetheless they did not engage in any more similar confrontations amongst themselves that I was aware of.

At times Sammy and his Daddy would go running early on a Saturday morning. They would go running around the Baisley Park Pond, which was not far from our building. Victor now also was in the Boys Scouts. He enjoyed going on weekend trips with the youth leader in the YMCA, which had their meetings in the youth center of our Building complex. Glen was not quite old enough to run with his older brother and perhaps not as venturesome at this time. He hung back, always contented with his plastic cars and army soldiers his Grand Mommy kept him supplied with. Glen was a healthy well adjusted lovable lad at the age of eight and nine years. Grand Mommy also enjoyed reading him Bible stories and he enjoyed listening with his round pudgy face and banjo eyes. Valerie loved to chase behind her brothers, and she tried to be and take part in all their games and play. But this did not always work for Valerie, because she also had her dolls and stuffed animals she loved dearly. She said she wanted to be a kindergarten teacher when she grew up, and I believed her as I watched her play school with her dolls and stuffed animals. I observed her growth and development and knew my Valerie would grow into a special caring person.

Sammy was becoming a brainy strong willed young man. He did not take anyone's word for anything. Everything to him had a cause and a response and he was about to search out these enigmas for himself. He belonged to the Public Library and in his early teens was reading on a college level. I did all I could do to encourage my children to follow their natural God-given talents. I took them to church, dressed in their Sunday best and lined them up in a row with myself setting on an aisle seat to observe them better. There the then Pastor Caesar now the venerable Bishop, expounded and explained the Gospel of Jesus Christ in words strong and clear, yet a baby could understand. There they received the true milk and meat of the word of God, which I knew would take them along the road of life.

Yes I was on the road of life with my four children traveling in an uncertain world. Mama had now moved back up in the Bronx to live and care for a lady she knew from the church who become ill. This was an elderly bedridden lady and now Mama's hands had found ways to be busy again. She visited us often and the children especially Valerie delighted in Grand Mommy's "time off". Daddy still lived in the old Bronx Apartment that I grew up in and it seemed as though there was a widening chasm between Mama and him. They were from a genteel generation, and did not flaunt their martial problems, if indeed there were any, and I did not pry.

We had promised Mama that we would take her to see the World's Fair in the spring of 1965. She never did make it to the Worlds Fair. Mama had been visiting with us for Christmas Holidays in 1964. We, that is Sam and I had discussed it with her, that she was always welcomed to live with us again whenever she became too tired of her baby sitting jobs, she said she would think it over. I rode halfway back home with Mama on the Boston Road bus on New Year's Eve day and kissed her good-by as she got off to catch the Tremont Cross-town bus. I was waiting for my Boston Road bus to take me back down to my Queens junction bus. As I waved and threw good-bye kisses to Mama, I did not realize that it would be the last time I would see my dear Mama alive in this world. Mama went to meet her Lord and Savior Jesus Christ, on Jan 1st 1965 at the age of sixty-seven years old just as peaceably and quietly as she lived her life here on this earth.

The lady who was sharing an apartment with her called me early on New Years Day. "Your Mother is ill, come quick and see about her." Sam and I left the children to care for each other and drove up in the Bronx from Queens to see about Mama. When we got there, the ambulance had already arrived and had taken Mama to Jacoby Hospital. Mama was in a deep coma. Her silver web hair had been opened up and pulled away from her face. They had examined her for any head wounds in case she had fallen. They had already taken x-rays. Mama had suffered a cerebral hemorrhage. The doctors wanted to go in her skull to open her up and stop the bleeding. I understood none of the medical jargon that the doctors were throwing at us. But Sam understood that these young doctors were medical students and eager to learn. I cried bitterly long and hard as I looked at mama's grey ashen face. I could not help her now. I touched her fingers under the covers, they were boney and cold. Little trickles of tears were streaming down her cheeks as I whispered in her ear. "Mama I love you, try to fight, Mama I love you". Even in Mama's impending death she was sorrowing for me who was uncontrollable at the time. The Doctors brought in a paper they wanted me to sign so that they could operate on her. Sam grabbed the paper and shoved it back on the bed. "Never, never will she sign for that;" he said. "She has a husband, let him sign." Sam got me out of the room away from the doctors. "I'll call your father, and I'll tell him not to sign." He looked at Mama and he knew that they had come to the parting of the ways. We three sat together in the waiting room; waiting as the doctor said for any change. Since we did not sign for any radical intervention, they started conservative treatments with Oxygen and

Intravenous medication. Somehow I did not do much praying as I can recall. I felt cold and alone even though Daddy and Sam were with me.

It was mid afternoon and I had not eaten anything. Sam went over to the vending machine in the spacious rotunda's waiting room, and brought me back coffee and a bun. He said, "I called the kids and they are alright and are praying for Grand Mommy.

I looked at Daddy, he was very pale and thin. For the first time I noticed that he did not have any hair at all on the top of his head, and that he had shaved his mustache off. He looked neither masculine nor feminine, but as a wounded creature. They were not together for a long time, living under different roofs, but they were always there for each other whenever there was a need. But now the separation would be final and I sensed the finality of it all. When we went back up to her hospital room, the nurses were with her, caring for her and adjusting her nasal gastric tube which had been inserted when we were gone. Mama's breath was coming now in short gasps and pauses. One nurse said as she was leaving the room, "Why don't you go home and get some rest and we will call you if there is any change. We knew we had to get back to the children and so we left Mama for the journey home in her white hospital gown. But her face had suddenly become placid and smooth. Her eyes were closed and she seemed peaceful.

I got the call from the hospital at exactly five minutes after six that evening as I was preparing supper, and Sam called Daddy to let him know.

Mama left us on January 1st 1965 at six P.M. The children were frightened and saddened especially Valerie who shared her bedroom when she lived with us. The funeral was simple with about fifty of her very closest friends and relatives. The missionary Ladies from the Bronx Community Church where we first worshiped, sang two of Mama's favorite hymns. Safe in the Arms of Jesus, and Face to Face with Christ my Savior. I was consoled in knowing that Mama was contented and happy now at last and was where she wanted to be. If given a choice she would not want to come back to this cruel world not even to be with her loved ones. She was with the one she loved the best, prayed to and sang praises to everyday. She was beautifully eulogized by the young minister who had taken over the Rev. Ellison's place. The service was not lengthy or strenuous, because her life spoke for itself. We laid Mama to rest on a cold winters' January day in the Silvermount Cemetery in Staten Island N.Y. Poor dear Mama I said to Sam as he and Daddy helped me and the children back in the Funeral Car for the trip back home. "We promised Mama a trip to the

Worlds Fair, and now she is in the fairest of all worlds."

Now I engrossed myself whole heartedly in the care and nourishment of my little family. Mama's sudden death left a hole in my heart, and I knew I had to fill that space up quickly, or I would not be able to contain myself. I could not cry easily, and the children seemed to be recovering sooner than I expected.

At the time, Dear Mother, Sam's mother was feeble and beginning to lose her eyesight. She stated to me one morning, when I went with Sam to visit her at her daughter's home, that she could only see shadows. She had cataracts but would not agree to an operation. This was not a dangerous procedure, but dear Mother was fearful and no amount of cajoling could convince her to have this eye operation, which would have improved her sight immensely. One morning about six months after Mama passed, Dear Mother said to me. "How is your Mother Muriel, I haven't heard from her in a long time." She used to call me up almost every week and we used to have such nice long chats together." "Have I done anything or said anything to her to upset her?" I was bewildered and amazed. I knew she was not able to attend the funeral but I did not know that her children had not informed her that my Mama had died. I looked over at her daughter Edith and she was shaking her head from side to side and was mouthing the words. "She doesn't know, don't tell her."

I was bewildered at first, but I mustered up some courage and I spoke quietly and kindly, "Dear Mother, my mother is O.K., she is fine, she is resting, and no you have not hurt her in words or in deeds." She sank back on her pillow and closed her eyes in peaceful sleep. It dawned on me then, what a blessed woman I was to have had two beautiful God fearing Mothers in my life, Sam's Mother, and my own. Her daughter Edith told me outside her bedroom "We try to keep all bad news from her." "Her heart is too weak and the Doctor says it would serve no purpose to give her something to fret over." I agreed and so Dear Mother never knew that Mama had passed. Quite a few people who she knew, including her younger brother Uncle Charlie died that year but the family kept it from her. Consequently every time I would visit Dear Mother, she would always say to me, "give your Mother my love and I hope she is resting well.

Now my Sam Sr. was always so busy in some project that he was engrossed in outside the home. He was now involved in the Flower Garden Contest. This was a citywide contest between all the Public Housing Projects in the City. Sam formed a Garden Club and called it the Uniteds. Each year the Uniteds entered the contest for the prize of the Silver Bowl or Golden Tray with the Stamp of the City of New York and the Mayor's Seal upon it. He had quite a few youths and senior citizens in this club, The Uniteds. Sam would start his Garden early in April; digging his ground in front of our building, making the earth ready for the planting of new seeds and young sprigs. He always envisioned his garden as a winner, and on the third try he won 1st prize. He received full recognition for his efforts, and was covered by the Daily News in the Sunday Edition with color photos of his Garden as 1st prize winner, and second and third place winners. I was happy and proud of him. He tried to stimulate competition in his children, but soon I noticed that it was becoming too much of an obsession for him to win. It seemed he must win at any cost, and the simple fun of gardening and watching things grow was lost. He spent money, time and energy into the gardens seeking recognition he felt would bring him satisfaction. I could not agree with him here. I was not looking for glory and praise from mortals because I knew this glory was only temporal. Nonetheless Sam worked his Garden with the help of his club members and Sammy and Vicky, hauling in plants and ferns to beautify his garden. And his gardens were really very beautiful. They were real works of art. People came from blocks around to see his Garden, and every year he copped either the 1st, 2nd or 3rd prize.

The days came and went swiftly, spring, summer, autumn, winter, the years were moving by fast like motion pictures. Sometimes I wanted to turn back the pictures on the screen of life and look closer. The older folks were passing, and the children were growing up and I was entering my middle years. I looked in the mirror more frequently now. Did I know the Muriel who was married to Sam raising his four children? There was little change in my face, and thank God I was still well and strong. But the thought occurred to me; the children will not always need me, and I will be left with time on my hands.

"Time, Time, please stand still for a short moment." "Let me get my bearings, so I can read the Signposts along the Highway of Life." Yes I was a traveler on the highway of Life, and every now and then I would encounter them, with their black directional arrows. I made up in my mind I was going to read those signposts, and try to govern myself and act according to the information indicated there on.

Some signs read, Winding Road up Ahead; Road Narrows; Stay in left lane; watch out for falling rocks. These were short intervals in my daily routine, when I allowed myself the luxury of quiet meditation. These moments were few but I could not put them aside altogether. And where was Sam in all these days? Busy! yes busy as a beaver, involved in the garden contest, his youth groups at the YMCA. He organized Dance groups and put on shows and plays for the Senior Citizens in our Neighborhood. I did not see him very much now, as he always had some meeting to attend with these various neighborhood groups. There was an Elderly lady named Mrs. Lasky who took a liking to Sam. She promised to introduce him to some of the big wigs in the Political world. And she did. Sam was now caught up in a swirl of meetings and telephone messages and debates. He seemed to be totally enjoying himself. The children and I were caught in the middle. I did not like the quiet evenings with my children around the dinner table, interrupted with telephone messages. I did not like this at all. I enjoyed the comfort and quiet of my little home when day was done, but Sam enjoyed the confusion of the outside world. Was I now seeing a side of his personality that I was unfamiliar with. Yes this appeared to be so. Yes he loved the limelight and the applause that he was receiving from his friends and associates.

The children became bewildered. Sometimes they did not know what to expect from him. It was clear from the beginning that I would not allow them to Dance on stage in any of the fund raising programs that he and his friends were supporting. The Dancers were young girls and scantily dressed. I felt his conduct was unbecoming for a married man and I told him so. Still he paid me no heed and continued his activities. There seemed to be a cold war going on between us now. He continued to do what he was doing and I stood my ground. I knew my main roll in life was to bring up our children in the fear and admonition of the Lord, and that did not include questionable dancing performances. Sometimes I felt I was fighting this battle all by myself, but I had the blessed assurance that God was on my side, and that he would never leave or forsake me. So I determined to pray and talk with my children everyday and point them in the right way of Salvation, because they each had to know Jesus for themselves. Having determined this, I kept my home together with Christ the head of the Home.

CHAPTER TWELVE

Resolutions and Realizations

Now the days were moving by fast. Tumbling over each other especially at summer's end and Sammy was preparing to enter in High School. Valerie and Victor who were the closest in age were close behind in Jr. High School. Glen was healthy and doing well in Elementary School. I had a few hours to myself everyday, after Sam left for work and the children returned home after three P.M. During this time, which was not really free time, I did all my cooking, cleaning, shopping, and surely all my household chores easily fit into these few free hours. I always felt that time was valuable, should be valued as money and not one minute wasted. This is why I always felt guilty when taking out a few minutes to relax and meditate. But I learned soon enough that it was profitable to take time out every now and then to just be quiet and unwind. I did not allow myself this luxury too often. Instead I visited the Library and began reading everything I could find time for. The children received good grades in school, and I visited with their teachers whenever there was an opportunity.

I was visiting dear Mother quite often now. She lived not far from us in Queens with her daughter Edith.

I was painting and drawing, and even thinking of going out to look for a job. Most likely a job in the art field, was what I had in mind. There were quite a few ads in the newspapers, looking for artists who were alert and talented and willing to learn new techniques. When I spoke to Sam about what I wanted to do he was furious. He said emphatically No! No! No! "No wife of mine will have to go to work, not as long as her children are still in school." "Case Closed." So it seemed the discussion was finished. I had no hard time finding things to do, and time did not lie heavily on my hands. I just could not seem to interest myself in old Lady Lasky's round of political meetings, and flower garden shows. This lady was also involved in the Queens Children Shelter. These children were a pitiful lot and some of them had no real family of their own. There were about twenty children in all who lived permanently at the shelter. Valerie went often with her father and especially on holidays to visit with them. She would help them celebrate their birthdays and decorate their dining area in the large downstairs playroom. I noticed that she was very much concerned with these poor unfortunate children, who did not have a home of their own.

Sammy Jr. was another one with a large heart. One Christmas he had saved enough money to buy his sister and brothers their Christmas gifts. But instead he bought presents for two little girls who he felt would be without on Christmas. They were two little girls that lived on the same floor of our apt building. They lived with their aunt. Their aunt had to go to work everyday to care for them, so consequently these little girls who were in their early teens had to look out for each other. They visited us often and I sensed a spirit of despair when we talked about Christmas around these children. The oldest girl Vera and the younger Veronica were only thirteen months apart from each other. The aunt wore a very gruff veneer and would barely speak to me when we met occasionally in the hallway of our building. Yet she was satisfied to know that her two little girls were over in our apartment when they were not in hers. Without any prompting on my part Sammy bought these two girls, two presents each, wrapped them himself, placed them under the tree and did not say who they were from. Victor was always carrying packages for someone. He would say to me so sincerely, Mommy I hope someone will carry your packages for you when I'm not around. What clear thinking, he had already understood the bible verse found in Ecclesiastes 11:1; Cast thy bread upon the waters for thou shalt find it after many days.

Valerie's favorite holiday was Easter. She loved the real Easter Story. Not the story with Peter Cotton Tail jumping around colored eggs. She knew the true meaning of Easter; how Jesus Christ went to the cross and gave up his life for the sins of whosoever would believe on him. She didn't care for the "Dressing Up" part of it as much as she enjoyed the Day, going to church and hearing the Easter Anthems. Indeed I had a lot to be happy and grateful for. Did I praise my children too much? I know now that I didn't; A little bit of praise is good for everyone. Was I an over jealous mother? I think not. I saw the potential of goodness in each of them. I saw good in all the children around me. I loved planning little picnics in summer, and afternoon snack times in the fall for them. The boys each had their own special chums, and Valerie had her girlfriends she palled around with. I saw now that it was more profitable for me to stay at home and be there for the children when they came home from school. We played checkers and scrabble games with each other and the neighborhood kids knew they could always get a mug of hot chocolate in winter and a cool cup of Kool-aide in summer.

Sam appeared bored with the family and me during this time. He seemed to be always looking for something else different outside the home to do. If it was not the flower garden contests, then it was the Queens Children's Shelter or the Political Scene. I felt these activities were harmless and self rewarding to Sam, but I felt they were occupying too much of his Family's time. But I did not harass him. I decided to stay close to the Home Fires and keep close watch on my family. I realized their teen years were very important and impressionable and that they needed close supervision.

Sam had a job in an Industrial Plant on Long Island. He said he needed to unwind on the weekends. Quite often he would pack a shopping bag with a change of clothes and take off to Staten Island to spend time with his older brother Jimmy and his elderly Uncle Charlie who lived on Staten Island. They would get up early and go fishing, or just sit around Uncle Charlie's kitchen and chew the fat with a bunch of his old cronies. I said to my husband one Sunday evening when he returned, "when you are away on your unwinding trips, your children are growing up and away from you." He gave one blank stare. This did not faze him in the least. Valerie went with her Daddy on some of his fishing trips. She seemed to enjoy these events thoroughly and I was glad for the both of them. The boys helped their father in his flower gardens getting up early, often times before sunrise, to dig, plant, and water the plot of ground allotted to us under our kitchen window. They were not enthusiastic at all because these chores sometimes lasted past mid-day on a Saturday, which they considered their play day. I would watch them from the kitchen window. The gardens were truly beautiful and flourishing under Sam's "Green Thumb." Sam bought them everything new for school from school supplies to school clothes when summer ended. He always provided a nice Holiday Table for his family for Christmas and Thanksgiving. Yet I sensed his restless moods and wandering spirit. He was not a contented man. I tried to reach him. I asked him what he was searching for. He did not realize his own discontent, so then how could he solve his problems. I believed within myself that he did not have the fullness of God reigning in his life, and without the presence and direction of the Lord Jesus Christ, life can be very uncertain at its best. I knew he needed much prayer to under gird him. The black man did not have any easy way to go back then in the 50's and 60's. In the 1960's women were still very passive. Although a glimmer of light was beginning to shine through on the feminist movement. I was not interested in such new ideas. I was not a woman looking for equal rights along with her husband. I was contented to remain in the home with my family. Sam and I did not discuss this equal rights between us. This was not our problem. It took me years to understand our problem, and it had nothing to do with the current issues of the day. Or did it? Was it because my Sam was a black man trying to make it in a society of white men. He was the only black man on his job. I don't believe now as I think back that he was receiving fair treatment as an intelligent person, because he was a black man. I listened intently to the discussions he had with his brothers. He was receiving unfair treatment and was poorly paid for the work he was doing. He was doing the work of three men but receiving salary for one. He was using brawn as well as brain. He would come in early on his job and leave late, and had to always fight for compensation. When he finally organized the men on his job and brought in a union, he was penalized. He became Shop Stewart and from then his job position was in jeopardy. There was always some sort of conflict going on between management and workers. Sam did not confide this in me. I gleaned this by overhearing his telephone conversations with his brothers and some of the other workers. I stood in the "wings" and I waited and watched. He was a pressured mal-treated black man underneath the mask that he wore. Why else was he so distraught and nervous every morning before going to work? He would sometimes complain of heartburn and stomach cramps. He had bouts of constipation and diarrhea. At times I became really frightened, thinking he was very ill. Sam went to the Doctor to be evaluated. The Dr. placed him in the hospital to rule out ulcers. After a week of testing, they found everything to be normal. He was just a nervous over-wrought man which was job related, and I did not realize this at the time.

Thank God I knew how to pray. Although I did not know what I was praying for, or what I was up against, I knew that my family needed divine intervention. My children needed their father in the home and so did I. So I kept the doors of my mouth shut and looked up to my heavenly father to be the under girding of our little family.

At this time Daddy decided that he wanted to move from his Bronx Apartment. So he took a smaller three room apartment in mid-Manhattan near the Yankee Stadium. He was just as spry and young as ever. He now was able to pursue his Tailoring jobs after retiring from the N.Y. Central Railroad System. He never considered Tailoring as work but as a peaceful outlet.

We kept in touch with Auntie Bertie and Uncle Rob who were still living in Brooklyn. Both of them were becoming infirmed now, and it was either Arthritis or Allergies that kept them close to home. When they did get out they would go together and it would be a day's excursion. Sam and I went to visit them often and almost always found one of them ill. There little apartment on the top floor was too hard for them to climb everyday, so consequently they could not get out often to get to the store. We would shop for them before coming over, bringing in the things they said they needed. I noted after a while their apartment was becoming cluttered, dark and musty, and neither of them wanted to venture out into the fresh air. Whether it was from the long haul up the stairs or just from habit, I do not know, but I realized they were becoming hermits in their own environment. Aunt Bertie was becoming very suspicious of everything and everyone. I wondered if this was evidence of advancing age. But Uncle Rob was still his jolly self and did not have an insincere bone in his body. They kept pictures of everyone around their living room and on every available surface, as far back as their Grandparents time. The pictures had faded to a brown hue and looked as though they would fall apart if they were blown on, or dropped. I suggested placing these pictures in an album for Aunt Bertie, but she said she loved looking at her family and relatives everyday and have them smile back at her. They had books, newspapers and magazines that they kept stacked up in almost every corner. Some of the neighbors in their building called them kooky but I called them Historians. They were my Auntie and Uncle, who were kind and caring to Jeanie and I when we were young and just cracking out of our shells, and I loved them both dearly.

I used to think to myself, how uncanny it is that Aunt Bertie and Uncle Rob, and Daddy all from the same era of time were so unlike each other in so many ways. What made the difference? Daddy was so young and spry for his age and these two, were feeble and dependent on each other.

Mary, a cousin on my mother's side, came from Bermuda often to see Aunt Bertie. Mary knew some friends in Brooklyn and often spent weekends with Aunt Bertie and Uncle Rob during her New York stay. Mary at this time was not an old lady, but very eccentric. She never traveled anywhere without bags and baggage. Before the label of bag lady was coined, I always thought of Mary as such. She always carried about with her gifts and packages, already wrapped, for anyone who might be celebrating a birthday or some other special day. Thus Aunt Bertie and Mary became bosom friends. Mary would air out, clean Aunt Bertie's apartment, shop for her, and see that Uncle Rob got to clinic if his appointment fell due during her stay.

Mary was a fantastic little trooper, and had won many awards given to her by The Nursing Brigade in Bermuda.

As Mary grew older she developed a hearing problem and had to wear a hearing aide, but she did not always have it turned on. Also Mary would fall sick while she was out in the street. She would feel dizzy and sometimes black out. When we knew she was here in the states we were always kept on the alert, fearing when or where she would have her next episode. I did not understand Mary's medical problems until I attended Nursing School, and ironically, I myself was also diagnosed with the same malady that Mary suffered from, but thank God I never fell ill in the street or when alone. This sickness is called Meniere's disease, which in simple words means an imbalance in the fluids in one of the eardrums. If too much fluid collects in one eardrum then an imbalance occurs and the person become nauseous and dizzy which is a devastating feeling. My doctor told me this problem was not life threatening, and to thank God it was not diabetic or some other debilitating illness. I simply must take my medication regularly, watch my diet, and stay on a low sodium diet, and to monitor my blood pressure. Well all told, Mary and I had a lot in common, and especially the fact that we both loved Aunt Bertie dearly.

But Daddy was tricky, and I had not realized that his flamboyance was just a cover-up for his loneliness. He suddenly announced to us one day when Sam and I were visiting him in his tiny mid-Manhattan apartment. "I'm thinking about getting married again." My eyes widened, and my mouth dropped open. It did not ever occur to me that Daddy would need another person in his life after Mama. I responded quickly. "Who but who would you marry?" He answered quickly, "Someone I always knew and loved even before I knew your Mother." Oh that was a sharp knife that went right to my heart. "How could he be caring for some one else and still be with my mother." I sat in silence with my hands dropped lifeless in my lap. This was a hard question and I knew it had to have a hard harsh answer. "Could one person love two people at the same time?" In that short moment of realization of what Daddy had just said I began to fathom it out. He was caring for someone else the whole time he was living with Mama, Jeanie and I. That is why they lived quietly together without demonstration and with a great gulf between them.

I ran in the bathroom, and splashed cold water over my sorrowing eyes. I looked in the mirror as I dried my eyes; I saw my mother's face looking back at me. Oh Mama, Mama, I whispered, "You poor angel from God, How you suffered in silence all these years.

CHAPTER THIRTEEN

Expanded Family

I realized soon that it was the best thing for me to remain at home and not to go out to work. Even though the children were well behaved and in good health I understood they had to be monitored at all times. Sammy now in his mid teens was noticing the girls or they were noticing him. Vicky at a young age was always planning field trips with the youth groups at the Y.M.C.A. Glen was now allowed to ride the public transportation with his bus pass. He got every other half Wednesday off to attend the Allergy Clinic to get his allergy shots. He was looking well and feeling good and I knew soon he would be clipping the apron strings. I insisted no longer that he wear a red cap so that I could identify him among a crowd of kids on their way home from school. Glen liked tropical fish and so did Valerie. Sam introduced them to the hobby of caring for all kinds of tropical fish. The job was time consuming but rewarding. They brought all kinds of guppies and angel fish to fill their big sixteen gal tank, which they kept in the living room. The big fish tank had a multi-colored light behind it which gave it a eerie allusion and it rivaled the light from the T.V. screen many an evening when the children waited in front of the bowl for one of the female fish to birth her little ones.

To tell the truth each one of my four children were quiet and obedient children when each were by themselves. But I needed much grace and patience when they were all together under one roof for any period of time. This proved true whenever I chose to celebrate their birthdays with themselves and a few of their chosen friends. Each was allowed to invite one of their friends so it was always at least eight children around the table enjoying someone's birthday celebration. During these days I noticed an undercurrent of competition amongst the four of them. Who was the smartest who was the greatest? Who sang the best, which ran the fastest? A strong element, which I thought unhealthy, was emerging between them. I argued with myself the good of competition. Yes it was a great tool when it was used as a tool to spur one on to attain his greatest capabilities but not to stir up discord and rivalry among siblings. This too I had to watch and find a way to guide and teach them a lesson here. Another year was winding down and a new one was knocking on our door. What was to be the watchword of this coming year? I used to be able to go to Watch Night Service when I was much younger and unhampered with noisy squirming children. But of late we had stayed at home and would bring in the New Year with pots and pans and whatever noisemakers we could improvise. Mama had passed on a New Year's Day so New Years day had a special meaning for me. But on this occasion I felt I had to do something memorable for the children since we could not all go out at night and celebrate together. Sam always went out with his brother Jimmy on New Years Eve to his Uncle Charlie's house in Staten Island so I was left with four noisy energetic teenagers. I made hot chocolate with marshmallows and tiny jelly and bread squares. We had peanuts and potato chips and pretzels. I allowed them as much free wheeling fun and frivolity as I thought was feasibly possible. My little girl Valerie was right along with them. She hung in their right along with her brothers and how she longed to be just like them. When the clock said a quarter to twelve, I made the four of them kneel down to pray. Each one had to say a little prayer thanking God for taking them through the past year and allowing them to see another one. They had done this many times before and each had their own little prayer time before they went to bed every night. But I wanted this occasion to be significant. When they were finished with the prayers, I pulled out the four kitchen chairs into the center of the living room. I made Valerie sit down in the first chair and lined the boys up next to each of the other three chairs. I filled a basin half full of lukewarm water, got a piece of soap and a cloth and towel and beckoned to Sammy first. Wash Valerie's feet Sammy, I spoke quietly. He looked at me intensely. He did not understand. He received no signals from my expression but the plain message that I was about to convey. Valerie started to giggle but one look told her I was serious. I said calmly and quietly, you must learn to love and respect each other. Sammy knew when his mother was serious and did not intend to buck against me when he recognized my intentions. He bent down and washed and dried Valerie's feet. Victor and Glen followed suit. Then Valerie in turn washed and dried Sammy and Vicky and Glen's feet. The boys in turn washed each other's feet. Before it was over we had a good old-fashioned feet washing service with water all over the floor and everyone laughing and screeching. But I'm sure the lesson was learned that New Year's Eve night. The lessons taught were humility, love and caring for each other. Not one to think himself more highly than the other. No matter what their station in life would be I wanted them each to respect the other without comparison or competition between them because they were sister and brothers. They got the message that night without exhortation and preaching and I must say I have not ever seen that maligned head of malice rise up between them ever.

The days coming and going swiftly as a weaving needle left me little time for reflection. There was always something to be done or accomplished. Sammy now in his junior year in high school was worrying over what college to apply to. I wanted him close to home. His father thought an Ivy League college on Campus would be best for him. We did not have much money between us. I thought again of taking a job somewhere. I heard of a few openings for Teacher-aide assignments in the Public School system and I planned to apply for an assignment. Sam did not protest when I broached the subject so I took this as a "go" signal. The Friday morning that I was scheduled for an interview, Glenny woke up feeling sick. He had been doing well all along with only occasional episodes of mild wheezing usually when he had the sniffles. The Lord had definitely touched his body and along with his clinic visits now once a month I felt he was relatively well. Well Glen had a full fledged asthmatic attack that morning. He became so ill that I had to take him to the allergy clinic for emergency shots. I saw my prospective job take wings. Well nothing was promised to me and I could not fault Glenny in anyway. I thought to myself maybe the timing was not right. Maybe the children were not ready for me to leave the home as yet. I appraised myself. I am still a young woman and I will have my chance. But where will Sam get the money for Sammy's college education. But something quiet within me whispered, "Be still and know that I am God" "I have never forsaken you yet" and I will not leave you now. So with this assurance I put again my desire to work on the outside on the back burner and continued in the home.

There was never an idle or dull moment in our home. Homework to be done PTA meetings to attend in four different schools. The children always took part in plays. One year Vicky was a huge letter in the George Washington's Day program. Glen on one occasion played Tiny Time in the Charles Dickens's Christmas carol. Sammy was be coming very professional in his trumpet lessons and I was very thankful that his father encouraged him in sticking with his music lessons even though the Master Galgano was a very exacting music professor. I wondered at times about my own education. I only had a high school diploma. For most women during the 1950's and 1960's this would have been enough especially with a family to rear. But I always felt there was more for me to learn and certainly it was. I now found myself becoming very interested in medicine and anything to do with the health field. I always did enjoy taking care of sick people and received a measure of satisfaction when they recovered. I went to the Library and took out books on basic Nursing. An Idea was brewing around in the back of my mind. Prepare yourself now for some future opportunity for higher learning. I advised myself and so I did.

One morning I woke up not feeling well at all. I had a headache and my stomach felt queasy. The feeling persisted for a few days then disappeared. I busied myself with my chores and my books. I decided to keep my desire to myself until I was fully able to pursue my desire. In the meantime I would bone up on vocabulary and math skills to make my entry into nursing school less stressful. I understood I would have to take an entrance exam in any of the local Nursing Schools. Indeed I had something great to look forward to. But God had other plans and directions for my life at this particular time. I soon discovered that I was carrying my fifth child. I was totally surprised and Sam was non-plussed. But underneath my outward expressions I felt a warm glow. I was happy and pleased that God had chosen me one more time to bring a little one into his world to train and nurture in the fear of the Lord. I was fruitful again at the age of thirty eight. I felt well and strong, but understandably Sam was worried that the baby might not be perfect because we were older parents. Here is where I stood firmly on the promises of God, one of which I repeated over and over again to myself and to Sam that "All things work together for good to them who love the Lord."

When I told the rest of my little family they were abashed, Sammy and Valerie understood almost immediately that changes would take place in the family setting. I would not be going out to work now at all, not for a long time. Glenny understood he would no longer be the baby in the family, and Vicky hoped for another brother he could play with. I was already three months pregnant when I decided to investigate that early morning queasy feeling especially after drinking coffee. I had this notion in the back of my mind, but I did not want to own up to the possibility of it being so; so soon because then I would have to prepare and plan and become the focus of attention in the family. And that is exactly what happened as soon as I told the children that they soon would have a little sister or brother. Sammy who was now in his senior year in high school became a quiet soft spoken young man. I never needed to ask him twice to do any thing at all for me. He would be riding home on the school bus and see me coming down New York Boulevard with the shopping cart and he would get off at the next stop wait for me at the corner and pull the cart home for me. Valerie and Vicky now helped me with the laundry. They each had their own little pile of clothes ready, socks matching each other and colors and whites separated the way I had been trying to get them to do all along. Valerie suddenly became very feminine. She no longer hung around her brothers but was interested in becoming the beautiful young girl that I knew she was. I was blessed I did not have to carry heavy during the hot summer months. But I did have to trek back and forth to school to visit the teachers during September and October as I usually did for the PTA meetings and required Parent-Teacher conferences. After the initial visits I forewarned them if I had to make another visit because of behavior or poor work that I would make an example of them in the classroom. Everything ran smoothly now as never before. Homework was always done now before supper and the T.V. Each one took their turn in clearing away the supper dishes and washing and drying without any squabbling. Even though Glenny was eleven and a half years old, he resorted to biting his nails and I said little about it because I knew it soon would pass.

Sam said very little as he watched me gain weight. One day he said to me, did you plan to have another baby or was it an accident. I looked him straight in his eyes and I said "Man may have accidents but God makes no mistakes."

That year Sam out-did himself in the N.Y.C. Housing Garden Contests. His garden the United's won 1st prize in all the five boroughs in N.Y.C. What a happy and proud man he was and I was happy for him. He won a silver plate stating 1st prize winner to the Uniteds. The Daily News Camera people came to our home and pictures were made of the Garden Club standing around the garden. Sam took a day off from work for the occasion and the pictures appeared in the color section of the Sunday News. All his work and efforts finally paid off, He truly had a green thumb. That same year before my last baby was born Sam's oldest brother Jimmy broke his leg and it had to be put in a cast. He went out fishing early one Saturday morning with some of the old cronies that he and Sam visited on Staten Island. They had a boating accident and the boat capsized. Everyone was rescued but Sam's brother, because of the heavy leg cast, he sunk immediately in the deep waters. This was almost too much for poor old Uncle Charlie to bear; he suffered a heart attack soon after and died. These tragic events followed almost one behind the other. We could not tell Dear Mother that her younger brother Charlie and Jimmy had died as this too would serve no purpose. Now in her eighties she could not move around so readily. She often asked for my mother and now she would enquire almost daily, "How is my brother Charlie doing, and why doesn't Jimmy call anymore?" I thought to myself doesn't life have so many strange twists to it. Here we were years ago, worried about Dear Mother's heart and she now has outlasted quite a few of her friends & family.

Daddy called me one day to tell me that he had set a wedding date. Yes he was really getting married and I knew the person well. He had only given me one weeks notice so I could not plan to attend the wedding. After the wedding he planned to move into the lady's home in New Jersey. I said to myself Daddy is actually moving away. He will not be by himself any longer and I will be happy for him. Time and events were moving swiftly. You cannot hold it back I thought to myself. We must take advantage of each fleeting moment because you never know what the next day will bring. These thoughts ran through my head everyday and I verbally thanked God for every precious minute that I had with my family.

The children were growing up and out of the way, but I would have a new little one to hold in my arms. Sammy had chosen a few colleges that he was going to apply to for acceptance. Victor was now going to the High School of Art and Design in Manhattan. Valerie and Glen were now attending Springfield Gardens High School in Queens. I hated the thought of Sammy going to another State to further his education but he had to make the choice. I was beginning to grow larger everyday now. I attended the pre-natal clinic in the Queens hospital center. The doctors said I was healthy and well despite the fact I was in my late thirties. I reminisced to myself. The words of the doctors after giving birth to Valerie. I should be careful not to have anymore children. They didn't think my heart was strong enough. But along came Victor and Glen after Valerie and without any complications, which proved the doctors wrong. I knew God had the last say in everything and I trusted him now to bring me through this pregnancy without any problems.

One morning early as I lay next to Sam between sleep and wakefulness and unusual thing occurred. There is no one in this world can refute this phenomenon. I know that Sam was asleep because of his heavy breathing. I felt my baby make deep turns and pushes within me. I laid my hands on my hard extended belly and began to pray silently. I asked God to bless my baby before she was born and to guide her all the days of her life. From deep within me I heard my unborn baby cry, just as clear and unmuffled as if she were in my arms. I sat up quickly and called out to Sam shaking him violently. Did you hear it? I cried. Did you hear what I heard? Heard what he said staring at me in bewilderment. The baby just now cried. It actually cried before it is born. "Oh Sam the baby cried." Well at that point Sam really thought that I needed some peace and rest. He said, "No that's your imagination." "You stay here." "Stay in bed a little longer, you don't have to make me breakfast and I can fix my lunch." He appeared tired as he left our bedroom. Soon after he left for work, Valerie came in my bedroom and said Mommy do you want me to stay home from school today? "I don't mind missing my math and gym class." She looked sad and apprehensive at me. Her father must have told her to keep an eye on me. But I was not imagining what I had heard and if I live to be 100 yrs old from the time of this writing I will not forget the voice of my tiny babies cries before she was born. I made my thirty ninth birthday on the fourth of January and my second little girl made her entrance on the 18th of Jan 1967 two weeks after my birthday. What a beautiful perfect child she was 7 lbs 12 ounces deep pink skinned with downy black hair. How proud and happy Sam was as if she was his first **and** only baby. We named her Edythe Joanne after her two grandmothers. When she was just two weeks old we took little Edythe over to Dear Mother's for her initial outing. Sam's mother said I cannot see her very well but she smells beautiful. Everyone was proud and elated over little Edie as they now began to call her. She was round and plump and perfectly healthy in every way. Valerie especially was happy with her new little sister. She confided in me weeks later, "Mommy I prayed every night for a little sister." I just don't think I could have made it with another brother." There was only one problem with little Edie that we soon discovered early on. And it was this. Edie did not stop crying, unless she was held, fed, played with or bathed. She did not like nap time, or crib time and if she was very sleepy and cried herself to sleep. She would wake up with angry squalls, because she cried herself to sleep. We thought this all very funny at first, that such a small sweet little bundle of pulchritude could be so uncanny. After a while I felt she should be especially examined by her pediatrician in the baby clinic. The doctor scrutinized her carefully and having received her shots up to date gave her a clean bill of health.

I took Edie to our church Bethel Gospel Tabernacle on the then New York Boulevard in Queens and there she was offered back to God, anointed with blessed oil and prayed over by three Ministers. She was pink and glowing in her long lacy dress at the age of six months with all her family around her snapping pictures. Such attention this one little baby was receiving I thought to myself, more than what my other four altogether ever received. How a mother's mind goes round and round, always remembering and cataloging the events in her family's history. This little bundle of joy I pondered, Oh God help me, why does she cry so much.

We had Edie's christening reception on the same Sunday in which she was blessed. Quite a few friends and relatives arrived for the event. We served sliced turkey and ham, and salad and punch and different sodas. Dear Mother was able to attend, her daughters having dressed her and rolled her into our apartment in her wheelchair. She was so happy and pleased to be present at such an occasion even though she could not see very well.

Daddy was not able to attend. Living now in New Jersey with his new bride he favored to make his presence scarce which was not unusual for him. Daddy was never a people person.

Aunt Bertie and Uncle Robert ventured out from Brooklyn accompanied by a younger sister in their church by the name of Mother Marcus. Mother Marcus had became their self appointed care taker and I was glad seeing that they were an elderly couple and needed someone to take an interest in them. I was amazed at how Aunt Bertie resembled Mama when she was now dressed in her lace finery. The same skin coloring and white hair. They were definitely two different persons but the family resemblance was very noticeable. This was quite evident when Dear Mother arrived in the living room in her wheelchair.

Aunt Bertie looked up from her cushioned chair that I had made ready for her and said. "Oh Sam's Mother, I have been thinking about you and praying for you."

Dear Mother raised her sightless eyes and said "O Sister Joanna I have been wondering about you, I haven't heard from you in so long." "How have you been?" Tears of joy welled up in her eyes, I can't see you very well she continued but I can hear your voice. Both ladies clasped each others trembling hands in friendship. Aunt Bertie happy to know that she sounded enough like her dear deceased sister to fill another need for friendship and did not deem it a sin to play the part to the fullest. The moment was not planned; the scene unrehearsed and Dear Mother was made happy to hear and be with her dear friend once again and Aunt Bertie was fulfilled in knowing that she helped to make it possible.

CHAPTER FOURTEEN

New Changes
and
Arrangements

Sammy was accepted at Parson's College in Iowa to his great pleasure and my consternation. My firstborn was leaving home, but I realized he had to try his wings in new surroundings. He was a good scholar and I trusted him to make good judgments. Sammy was invited to come out to the college earlier, to take some preliminary courses in order to make the transition to campus life much easier. His father flew out to Iowa with him and stayed a week to get him settled in his Dorm room. The ties were cut now and Sammy had to put to test for himself all the principles that he had learned since early childhood.

Vicky was doing well in the high school of Art and Design but I sensed restlessness about him. He always had wandering feet and I felt that he wanted to make a move now. He and his father talked long and hard and it was decided that Vicky would finish High School, find a job in his particular Art field. Glen was now in a work-study program; working and earning one week; going to school and learning the next. This suited Glen's easy going jovial personality very well. Valerie was a gem doing well in High School and especially so in Driver's Ed. She was the first of the siblings to receive her drivers' license at seventeen. How proud I was of my "pinky toes" with the southpaw. Little Edie was happy, healthy and quite energetic. Much strength was needed to keep up with her, especially when she discovered that feet were made for walking. She did not like her playpen and only tolerated the stroller for outings in the park. Everyone was at her beck and call and sorry to say I knew I had a spoiled baby on my hands, but I could not and would not compare her with her sister and brothers. They were so much older than she and they had each other. They cared for her and played with her, but they each had their own special activities that did not include a little sister. The closest in age to Edie was Glen and they were almost twelve years apart. So she was destined to be a lonely little girl and so she set out to make her presence recognized at all times.

I watched her grow and marveled how she captivated everyone's heart with her innocence. I was determined also to train this little girl as I so did the others to love and respect themselves and to love and honor God.

Time never stands still and the tides of life wait on no one; and as the seasons follow each other in succession, so does life and death.

Dear happy fun-loving Uncle Rob fell ill soon after Edie's christening celebration. Aunt Bertie was lost and in a quandary. They had married early in their beloved Bermuda and had been together so long, how could they bare to be separated now. So many years of loving and abusing fighting and accusing had passed. They had one son named Willie, a robust man the image of his father living somewhere in the five boroughs.

He had three living wives, so he in order to dodge each of them, he was forever moving about. Aunt Bertie searched him out, having not heard from him in many years. She felt he should know his father was ill. Mother Marcus, Aunt Bertie's bosom friend came upon him in one of the churches she attended. He was a self ordained minister which was questionable having three living wives with a flock of silly women as followers and no church building of his own to preach in. Their son, the Reverend Willie Burtcher, was a quest speaker in the little mission church where Mother Marcus attended and she recognized him from the picture Aunt Bertie had of him on display in her apartment. When he was informed that his father was ill in the hospital, he promised to see them both right away. This gladdened Aunt Bertie's heart for Uncle Robert was a very sick man in fact he had terminal cancer. Willie came to see them on one occasion and then once again when he visited Uncle Robert in the hospital. But Uncle Robert could barely respond to his long lost son because he was so weak. Willie was not a young man and should have been living a much more stable lifestyle, but he must have deemed it more important to continue his activities than to see about his parents. Uncle Robert lay sick for one year and Aunt Bertie remained faithful to the end, hobbling about on her walking stick to see about her Rob with Mother Marcus at her elbow.

He died at the age of seventy five with Aunt Bertie at his side. She did not whimper and she did not mourn and during the whole time of the preparation of the funeral, she verbally berated him for not taking care of himself not eating the right foods although she cooked every bit of it and served it to him. She scolded him outright in the Undertaker's parlor when Sam and I went to view his body before the service. She fussed with him for leaving her alone with all the responsibilities of the funeral. If it were not such a sad occasion it would have been ludicrous. She stepped back from his casket at one point and landed a thump with the flat of her hand square on his forehead. "You got your wish now Rob, you got your wish," she said, "You always wanted to leave me." Sam and I stayed close by her now along with Mother Marcus. We knew she was all torn up inside and this was the way she had of expressing her sorrow. We also knew that Uncle Robert was happiest when Aunt Bertie was feuding with him over some unknown sin. I could see him now as it used to be when Jeanie and I would visit them. He with a twinkle in his eye looking over Aunt Bertie's shoulder as she taunted him.

Sam must have read my thoughts because he said, "He's peaceful now and God rest his soul."

The funeral was held in one of the larger churches in Brooklyn. Uncle Robert belonged to several secret lodges and they sent him beautiful flower arrangements. Aunt Bertie was a long standing member in her church and they both were well known in the community. Uncle Rob was also an Air Raid Warden in World War II. The pitiful part of this tale is that their Minister son Will did not attend his father's funeral. I believe this hurt Aunt Bertie more than the actual death of her husband. Sam played the part of her son at the funeral services and no one was the wiser since no one knew him personally except Mother Marcus. Uncle Rob was well loved and reverenced by all who knew him but few tears were shed because we all knew and was thankful that he was released from his pain and suffering.

We watched the neighborhood crowd gather about the church steps as they placed the heavy coffin in the long grey hearse. Aunt Bertie stood at the top of the church steps and flung out her arms to the milling crowd. "Prepare to meet thy God" she cried out in shrill sentences." "Dust we are, and to dust we must return to the earth." Her slight bent body was trembling. Sam caught her by her arms quickly as her spindly legs buckled under her. We managed to get her down the steps and into her waiting car. A tired old lady she was, dressed in her finest black lace dress and wearing an oversized black Hudson seal coat that had seen better days.

What a brave lady she was, playing another part in another scene from life, unplanned, impromptu and unrehearsed. Uncle Rob's death took its toll on Aunt Bertie now.

She stayed in the apartment with curtains drawn letting in neither sunlight or fresh air in and refused to answer the telephone. Sam and I visited her often after the funeral to help her dispose of Uncle Rob's property. I knew it would take her a good while to adjust to the separation of her and her Rob. Does a spouse ever get used to the final goodbye?

Sammy promised us before he left for College, that if he needed anything he would write. I as his mother hoped he would be needing something every week so we could hear from him often. But Sam being a man felt differently about Sammy's statement. "If I need something I will write home." This did upset Sam to no end because every time we received a letter from Sammy, he did ask for things. He asked for heavy socks and insulated gloves for the weather was very chilly in Iowa during the winter months. He asked for denim jeans because no one wore dress clothes in college. Raggedy washed out jeans was just beginning to catch on in the sixties. We packed in little cans of sardines and tuna fish, little jars of jelly in each box we sent to him. Sam was glad that he needed so many things from time to time and it also meant that we heard from Sammy on a regular basis. He was doing well in his courses and passing with average grades.

The Vietnam War had now escalated and I was truly thankful that Sammy had a draft deferment and was ensconced away at college. Vicky was now chomping at the bit, and I felt he was waiting his turn to leave home. I sensed this wandering spirit in him again and made him promise that he would at least finish High School which he did without any problems as Vicky was a quick intelligent young man. Soon after he graduated from High School he joined the Navy. This was a big surprise to me for he was never one for conformity or regimentation. The days were now flying by swifter than a weaver's shuttle. It seemed I wasn't given a chance anymore to accustom myself to any one given situation before something new appeared on the horizon. Events just tumbled one upon the other from day to day. I pondered to myself, one day they are dependent adolescents, the next day they are vibrant young personalities finding their way in the world and making their own decisions.

In the meantime little Edie was making her own little strides and inroads into everyone's heart. Thank God she was well and healthy and never seemed to catch a cold when everyone else around her was sniffling and fighting off cold germs. But I realized one day that my little baby girl had a crying spirit. She was toddling around into her second year still crying and fuming when put down for her nap or made ready for bedtime. Her father insisted that she never be left to cry alone. If she would not get to sleep at night, someone must rock her to sleep. Sam bought a rocking chair just for this purpose. Consequently, Glenny and Valerie took turns in rocking Edie to sleep every night. I soon became very exasperated at this arrangement; somehow I felt little Edie was taking advantage of the situation; and she was and I knew that she was.

One morning as I was clearing away the breakfast dishes, and Edie was sitting close by me in her highchair; beating two large serving spoons together; an incident that occurred a few months before Edie had seen the light of day flitted across the recesses of my mind. Yes I had heard an infant cry, clear as a bell and as sure as if the baby was in my arms. That was my Edie crying, I thought to myself just as she cries now. I left the dishes and dried my hands and grabbed my darling little girl up in my arms and snuggled her close to me. I whispered to her quietly. "Edie baby don't cry so much, Mommy and everyone loves you dearly. She reached up for one of my ears to roll between her tiny baby fingers. This was her signal of contentment and would always reach for an ear as soon as she was picked up. Edie had an internal instinct that she was the last of the siblings and must have felt that she would grow up alone, and since this was so she manifested the need to be in company with someone at all times. I listened to the inner spirit within me, and marveled that I had not discovered this sooner. That my baby wanted love and assurance because everyone around her was so caught up with their own personal agenda's that they only had brief moments and swift hugs and kisses for little Edie. I played with my little baby girl the rest of the day and made sure that she had special time allotted out for her by everyone in the family regardless of their busy schedules. As a result of these considerations, Edie became a less fuming agitated little girl and became everyone's endearing little Edie.

We took Edie to see her grandmother Dear Mother very often now. Dear Mother could barely raise her head off the pillow and speak she was so weak and tired. Her doctor said she needed constant care. Her children did not put her in a Nursing Home or Hospital. Her daughter Edith decided she would take time off from her job and care for her mother. Dear Mother was very ill, her heart was tired of beating and she could not move herself so she had to be turned from side to side to avoid skin breakdown. Edith cared for her mother night and day and her brothers supported her. Finally after a long restless night Dear Mother closed her eyes in peace at the age of eight four.

The funeral was large and well attended. She was well known on Staten Island where she raised her young family. Folks came from far and wide to be with her family and to praise her God for her God fearing life. I noticed my husband Sam was especially touched. He voiced no sorrow and he did not cry but he wore a shroud of deep moroseness I found hard to penetrate. He threw himself into his work more intensely than before, working longer hours and weekends. He said he needed to work in order to have for the children, but I knew he did not want any time left to think about or feel the devastation of his loss. I tried to talk to him to be there for him but his whole personality did a complete turnabout. I understood now what an impact the pious life of his Mother had on him. I remembered now that at one time in our few discussions he had said to me that he trusted no one in this world but God and his Mother.

I read my bible everyday. I prayed and sang hymns to myself and found refuge in God's Holy Word. The Gospel songs gave me the uplift that I needed to keep me afloat from day to day. I now noticed an acute personality change in Sam. He became very argumentative with anyone and everyone at the drop of a hat. He was becoming an angry man. Who is he angry with? I questioned myself. There were times when nothing and no one could please him. I watched waited and prayed. This is another form of mourning I said to myself and so I marked time. But Sam continued in this vein after his mother's death and so I adjusted myself according to his moods. He was my husband and I loved him dearly even when he expostulated vehemently over some small inconsequential matter. I held my peace waiting for the storm to abate. The children noticed the change in their father also although no outward remarks were made. They would watch for the their Daddy's car to pull into the parking lot of our Project building, and called out "Red Alert" to each other. It took me a good while to understand what this signal meant. The only one who would get a ready smile and a gentle hug from their father was little Edie. Her waiting outstretched arms were his reward for a tired stressful day.

I understood later on that there were problems on his job and unfair dealings were in progress. Younger men with less experience were being advanced before him. They never forgave him for bringing the union shop into his plant; thus he was threatened in his job position. He was beginning to talk more to me now, opening up and I learned more about his job when he took me on the plant site. I saw the huge plant where he was Traffic Manager. I met a few of his immediate bosses. They all seemed pleased with him and his job performance, but I knew there was something definitely wrong here. I sensed it in the atmosphere. He was a good worker but they would not give him the salary he felt he was worth. He talked shop all the time now, with his younger brother Dan and myself. He constantly admonished the children everyday, to learn all they could and to go as for as they could go in their education. Sam was a very smart intelligent man and I felt he should have had a better chance to further his education when he was a youth.

One day Valerie came to me with a newspaper ad that she had cut out of the Daily News. The ad was looking for perspective Nursing students. The Helene Field School of Practical Nursing was looking for bright eager men and women interested in caring for the sick and disabled. Those who were willing to put their personal lives on hold for one year and train in the Helene Field School of Practical Nursing for a rewarding career and a chance to make a moderate salary. One had only to write a short letter to the school stating why he or she wanted to become a nurse and to request an application to fill out and send back. Valerie was eager with lots of encouragement.

"Mommy you always wanted to be a Nurse," she explained to me. "Just take a chance and see what happens." My mouth flew open, my daughter was serious. She really wanted me to go to school and become a nurse.

"But Valerie," I said, who will take care of Edie. "I will," she said. "I will take care of Edie during the day, and go to night school." "I don't know, I sighed." I have to think.

Valerie was in her senior year in High School. I thought it would be cruel to yank her out in her senior year. "I have to talk with your father about this," I said, "we both have to decide." When I did talk to Sam, he offered no defense. Surprised, I spoke to him repeatedly, before I finally sent out my letter to the Nursing School. They sent me back an application and I filled it out and sent it off immediately. I was soon called in for an interview. I had only to take a general information entrance exam, pass a physical and I would be on my way. I became very apprehensive and hesitant now. What was I thinking of how could I expect Valerie to put her education on the back burner while I pursued mine. But Valerie was eager for me to advance myself and pursue my dream of becoming a Nurse and she was so convincing.

So Valerie arranged to take evening classes three times a week, and Glenny promised to do all he could to help her in the care of Edie.

Edie was now all a glow. This situation suited her fancy immensely. She knew that Valerie and Glenny would be especially attentive and sensitive to her needs since her Mommy would be away most of the day. I found myself whispering again. "Time, Time, you are moving too fast. Stand still for just a little while and let me feel the moment." Dear God, please don't let me make a mistake. I studied everything I could for the General knowledge entrance exam, and passed it with flying colors. The physical was not as easy. The doctors discovered my heart murmurs, and advised me to go on a diet and lose weight. I agreed to monitor my health more carefully while caring for others. My main concern now was Valerie. How could I ever compensate her for what she was about to do? How does one know when or if he is making the right decisions or not. The answer to that question is that one never really knows for sure. We have to act on faith; and so I did; put my faith in God and moved on out in faith. My enrollment in Nursing School proved in the long run to be the right move for all concern. The nursing School was affiliated with The Hospital for Joint Diseases then located at 1919 Madison Ave in Harlem between 123rd and 124th Streets. The classes at that time in 1970 were held in a brick building on 119th St. and Madison Ave with most of the clinical work done on the floors of the Hospital itself. And so I entered a new phase of my life with cold hands and trepidation in my heart. I knew and understood it was going to be a long hard journey. To make a quiet unassuming person as myself into a self-assertive individual who would have the care and concern of others always foremost in my head heart and hands would be a tremendous task. But I was determined, God was truly able and Valerie was willing.

After visiting Aunt Bertie on Saturday morning we decided that she could not live alone any longer, in that top floor apartment. We talked to her, Sam and I, and had a hard time convincing her that she must come and live with us and our family. The problem was, we did not have much space, but we were promised a house to rent by the F.H.A. and was looking forward to having an extra room. We started packing some of her belongings and cherished bric-a-brac. She was not willing to leave behind a toothpick. Somehow her son Willie got a whiff of our plans and suddenly appeared on the scene and put a stop to this move. He must have thought that his mother gained from his father's death. But this was not the case. Nonetheless he stepped right in and gained his mother's confidence. He managed to get her to sign her meager savings over to him, in exchange verbal promises to care for her. Aunt Bertie in her sincerity and eagerness to have her long lost son near her now believed everything he said. We could not convince her that he had an ulterior motive. He moved his mother from her top floor apartment with all her furnishings to his dank three-room basement apartment in a very unattractive neighborhood in Brooklyn where she knew no one and no one knew her. We learned later on through many conversations with Mother Marcus that her son Willie had sold her television and her two radios and many of her other belongings with the explanation that he needed the money to pay her outstanding bills; which he stated she had let slide. This was a pitiful state of affairs but Aunt Bertie refused to believe that her son did not have her best interest at heart. They were estranged from each other for so long, and she seemed so pleased now at his attentions. No one could convince her otherwise. Eventually he closed off her telephone and we could not communicate with her at all. All the information that we received we gleaned from Mother Marcus. He could not deny this lady access to his mother since she was connected with his ministerial affiliation. But this man proved to be no man of the cloth but a wolf in sheep's clothing.

In the meantime I entered Nursing School along with forty-one other candidates for the class of 1971. Life for me was now a round of books, grafts, studying and more studying. We started classes at eight A.M. everyday and finished at 2:30 or 3 P.M. in the afternoon. But this was not the end of the day. There was always research material to be looked up and study groups to attend. Nursing School was to absorb my every waking hours and sleeping nights if I was to make the grade in a years time.

One day Sam came home from work and informed me that he was going to quit his job. He said he was tired of being used by his Corporation. They owed him so much he said and no matter what he could never please the Company. He appeared to be a very troubled man. I looked at him in disbelief. "How could anyone walk away from his job," I thought to myself. He looked at me, and he must have read my thoughts. "Don't worry," he said, we have enough to take us through a year, and I'll find something soon. My prayer list was growing longer now, as the days came and went. The children topped the list. Then Aunt Bertie was next. My studies and myself came next and now I added Sam and a job for him to my prayer list. It seemed I was always begging God for something. But whom else could I go to. Who else knew and understood my troubled spirit but my heavenly father. In the quiet time of the midnight hours I lifted my heart to him. "Dear God I whispered." "I cannot make this journey by myself." "Be with my children away from home." "Help me through Nursing School." "Undertake for poor helpless Aunt Bertie, and guide Sam in finding a new job." Undefined peace swept over my spirit. "My Father is rich in houses and Lands, this dear hymn came to mind. He holdeth the wealth of the world in his hands." "Of Rubies and Diamonds, Silver and Gold, His coffers are full, he has riches untold, and was I not child of The King.

CHAPTER FIFTEEN

The Task

It became clear to me and as evident as the nose on my face, that I had a great task confronting me. The task was to steer my family and myself through the forthcoming testing days. I realized early one morning as I was brushing my teeth, and inspecting them in the bathroom mirror, that the mantle of responsibility had fallen on my shoulders. Shoulders narrow and unaccustomed to burdens. The burdens that I was familiar with here-to for were ones I carried in my heart, and when they became unbearable I usually gave them to God. Now the time had come when I for-saw the need for physical and mental exercise on my part in maintaining my family in their different maturing stages.

With the help of the Lord I made plans, cut out the patterns, and now I must follow through.

Sam had always been the strong shoulders in the family, and rightly so. He, having been the breadwinner in the family, I never had the worry of unpaid bills or meeting the children's needs. But now Sam must look for a new job career, and I sensed this need of encouragement although never verbalized.

Sammy away at college wrote often now not always asking for things, as he promised his father "When I need something I'll write home." He wrote how the Black revolution movement was seeping through the cracks and crannies of this Ivy League Institution. There were two hundred and fifty black students in all among a population of at least three thousand students. Some of these students were organizing and trying to include a black studies course in the curriculum. They were looking for recruits and Sammy was targeted. Sammy wanted to remain neutral, but he could not straddle the fence. So eventually he had to involve himself in some of these activities. Unsavory persons were found among each faction. Guns were discovered on an instant during a surprise dorm check. The white students and the pitiful minority of black students were each planning a demonstration, each championing their own cause. But the guns were incidental; they had nothing to do with the demonstration of the black students. They were unloaded and kept for scare protection when the students shopped in town. The administration was not sure of any of the explanations for what they had found. So they decided to avoid trouble and publicity, understanding that the Black students were fighting for a chance to learn more of their own culture in a white society. Black pride was their watch word and perseverance was their emblem. They assembled in their meeting halls, and invited some of the black personalities of the day to speak for them. One personality was Congressman Stokes of Ohio. When Congressman Stokes arrived on the grounds, Sammy and two others were appointed tour guide around the campus grounds during their stay at the college. Eventually after much speech making, a Black Studies Program was implemented in the curriculum with the full recognition and consent of the faculty.

Much prayers and supplications went up for a new job for SWG; I was beginning to call him that now, in order to differentiate him from our son Sammy. He never liked being called Sammy now, after he had grown so tall and straight and had entered college. His siblings never ever hesitated in calling him Sammy; and I knew that deep down in my heart he would always be my young son Sammy. But he was now growing into manhood, so now I must modify my mothering toward him and call him Sam. Later on, or maybe I'll say just a few years later this adoption of Sam from Sammy became quite thank worthy, as he and I had to work under the same conditions, side by side in a professional atmosphere, Sam also became a Nurse, graduating with high honors, from the same Nursing School that I did, working in the same Nursing institution, side by side on the same critical care floor.

Thank God for SWG's younger brother Dan who had always been a businessman with a good head on his shoulders, who came to his brother's aid. He was the owner of several Parking Garages in the New York City Area, and he brought his brother SWG in the business as an equal partner.

I was pleased and thankful to God when this transpired. I understood that he could not any longer be under the jurisdiction and confines of private enterprise. This arrangement that he had with his brother was very satisfying to the both of them.

Two of my prayers had now been answered. Sam's college education had not been interrupted and SWG had found a niche for himself.

The next weight-bearing problem that I carried around with me was the future of Aunt Bertie. Was she truly suffering at the hands of her own son? I did not know for sure. But something was very peculiar here. I wrote her letters and had sent her greeting cards at her new address, and never received an answer. At this time she had no telephone, and I knew now the reason why. She had moved in with her preacher son because she was lonely. But Aunt Bertie had always paid her bills promptly. This was quite mysterious to me. So we decided, SWG and I would investigate. One Saturday SWG and I went over to her house where she was supposedly living with her son and knocked on her door. The apartment was at the end of a long dimly lit hallway. We heard the ferocious barking of a dog behind the door. The next came a few shuffling footsteps and then a very weak voice answered, "who's there?" I answered; it's me Aunt Bertie, its Muriel and Sam coming to see how you're doing. "Oh I'm okay was her whispered reply." I'm okay she repeated again, "but I can't open the door. Webster does not want me to open the door to anyone." "But why Aunt Bertie," I started with a catch in my throat. "Why can't we see you for a little while?" Her little weak voice came back as if repeating sentences recited to her. "Because the dog will run out and get lost and Wille needs the dog to protect his property. After a moment we turned around in dismay and started out the hallway, and as we were going we heard her faint voice call out to us. "Call me when you get home, don't forget now, ring me." These were always her last words she said to us, whenever we left her top floor apartment. "Ring me up." She didn't even realize at this point, that her telephone had been shut off.

There were some children playing on the steps outside the house. They must have heard the dog barking. They looked up at us curiously. You know that old lady that lives in that back apartment?" "Yes, we both answered in quick attention." "Well said the only girl in the group only about ten years old but eager with gossipy information that she had heard from her elders." "The preacher comes every night and takes the old lady and that ugly old dog out for a walk up the street. One of the little boys shook his head from side to side and said nobody dares to go near that dog. He's awful." Not only were my shoulders weighted down, but my heart was torn open for Aunt Bertie. I looked at my husband. "Sam," I said, "We've got to do something about this." There is some sort of crime here." "You cannot keep someone confined against their will." "Don't worry," he tried to console me as we drove home. "I'm going to look into this." When we returned home and I looked in the mailbox, there were two more unopened letters, and a Mother's Day Card I had sent to Aunt Bertie's new address unopened and with the Postmaster's Stamp "Unknown Resident" in bright red letters.

"This will never do," I said to SWG, "She doesn't even have a mailing address." "If I had not heard her weak little voice behind the door, I would think it all a dream." "I'm going to inquire" Sam said. "I will call the police." He was all take charge now. "Who is this man with a turned back collar, and what is he trying to do with your Aunt Bertie?" "He must have lost all his marbles" he grumbled to himself, "but guess what I still have all of mine."

Sam went to the nearest precinct on his next free day and filed a complaint against the Reverend Willie Burcher. They promised to investigate the case and to keep us informed. Within a few days we received a call from the precinct where we filed a complaint. It seemed as though two officers went to the apartment door without a search warrant and knocked and knocked just as we did, but Aunt Bertie would not open the door, even when they stated "Police here just to ask you a few questions." But they could not gain entry and could not force the door because they did not have a search warrant.

We talked this over together. Suppose there was no foul play, and Aunt Bertie appeared contented living confined behind closed doors with her son and making her own decisions. The chief officer at the desk stated that since all lines of communications had been cut off from her that our request for a search warrant was valid. All necessary papers were prepared and signed for and within 24 hours the police promised to do their job. Sam and I promised to be on hand to whisk her away in our car if the situation presented itself.

Sam and I informed the children that Aunt Bertie may have to come and live with us for a while. During the evening before the search when SWG, the children and I were discussing this matter, we received a phone call from Mother Marcus. Her voice was subdued but she sounded worried. " I went to visit Aunt Bertie", she said. Mother Marcus was able to get in after Willie tied up that dog. She continued, Auntie is in a bad way. She fell off her chair and it appears that her hip is broken. I warned her son if he didn't get help for his mother immediately that I would expose him to the Ministerial Conference that he belonged to. That changed his tune pronto. We wrapped her up as she was frail and wining and then hailed down a cab to take us to the nearest hospital emergency room. Poor Aunt Bertie was a pitiful sight and in a lot of pain. Mother Marcus rambled on and on. He's going to get his punishment for this ill treatment of his parents. Not attending his father's funeral and locking his poor demented mother away from those who cared for her. Well I certainly was relieved and told Mother Marcus how thankful I was that Aunt Bertie had such a dear friend as herself. "Twice kindred spirits we are," she said, a dear faithful friend she had been to me and we are sisters in the Lord. Another prayer had been answered, and without any intervention from mankind. Aunt Bertie certainly was in a lot of pain from a broken hip but she was in a clean environment where she would get all the care and attention that she needed. The doctors at the hospital advised us that Aunt Bertie was a strong feisty lady and could certainly survive the setback of a broken hip. She had been through an ordeal, not well nourished or cared for, and certainly in a very unsafe cluttered up apartment. The search warrant was called off, and Willie absconded the apartment taking his boxes and books and papers. The dog was led away to the ASPCA, and the apartment was given back to its owner. What a sad turn of events, I mused to myself. That Aunt Bertie had to come to such a disquieting end. She was not dead, and regaining her health and strength slowly each day. Within six months, her hip had healed with the help of the Lord and good nursing care and rehabilitation. She was now able to hobble about her hospital room with the assist of a folding walker. But the sad part was that Aunt Bertie did not recognize us anymore. There was no recollection in her tired eyes. She only smiled sweetly for us, as she did for her nurses and her other health care workers.

How merciful God is, I said to myself. She does not remember the injustices that were done to her. She does not remember the loss of her dear Rob. But when you mention the name of Jesus her eyes would light up for joy. "Oh yes she smiled to me one afternoon, as I sat smoothing out the wrinkles in her small bony fingers. "Oh yes I know Jesus, He's my best friend.

Nursing School was becoming more intense now. I found myself getting up earlier every morning, and staying up later every night in order to keep up with the assignments. Only the Lord knows how my Valerie was my constant standby. She took complete charge of little Edie, washing, dressing and feeding her everyday while I was in Nursing School. She took her down to the playground and let her romp around with the other little kids. We had to find a way to reward Valerie. She certainly was worth more than her weight in gold because Valerie was only about one hundred and twenty pounds at this time. So we decided, Valerie being an excellent driver as she was, we would give her, her first car. We could not afford a shiny brand new car. It would have to be a used car, something serviceable, and in her favorite color blue.

So when her birthday rolled around we really did surprise her. SWG and I bought her a blue umbrella and a birthday card. Then we really did surprise her when we pointed to her very own blue "67" Chevrolet parked outside on the curb. "My very own car?" she cried in disbelief. "I can't believe it!" What did I do to deserve such a birthday gift!" Her blue grey eyes growing big like saucers. "You were born to us, Valerie Dianne nineteen years ago, and have been a lovable obedient daughter, and that's reason enough." SWG was pleased that she was so happy. He set out right away to teach her the fundamentals in maintaining her car and she listened intently.

Glen at the age of sixteen was now the dependable young man in the house. When he arrived home each day, either from school or his work-study job, he would take over the care of Edie, leaving Valerie a little free time for her studies. It was upmost in mind, and very important to her father and I that Valerie receive her high school diploma with her classmates and that's what Valerie did. The courses she took in night school were credited towards the points she needed for graduation. We were very proud of such a young lady as our Valerie for she received her diploma after giving up a whole year of her life to care for her baby sister so that I her mother could attend Nursing School. It made me even happier when she announced that she intended to go to Medgar Evers College in pursuit of a career in early childhood education.

The task never diminished. It was ever before me. In the morning I awoke early to get on my knees with my petitions before my God, and it was the last thing I did at night when I gave thanks to the Lord Jesus Christ for being so mindful of me and my little family all during the day. My nursing school studies were becoming very tedious. Long hours spent in the books after attending classes during the day. This was very disconcerting to SWG. He could not understand why I had to study so much, and was becoming very disgruntled about it. He fumed and complained when I had to prepare for a test the next day. I tried to tell him it would all pay off in the end. "I'm waiting for it to end now," he fumed on many occasions. In the meantime, Sam was still away at college. Vicky had joined the Navy, and Valerie was making plans to study Early Childhood Education in Medgar Evers College. She was very good with younger children, and she certainly had enough practice with the care of little Edie. We learned later on when Edie was ready to enter school she was ahead of her class, already able to read simple words and sentences simply because Valerie had taken up time with her. Soon we enrolled Edie in the Nursery School across the street for a small monthly fee, and surprisingly she adapted very well to her new surroundings. My one desire was to see all my families' efforts come to fruition, and slowly but surely with the help of the Lord, things seemed to be working out for every one concerned.

Muriel Ratteray Green

Muriel Ratteray Green

140

CHAPTER SIXTEEN

The Glory and The Praise

Finally all the red tape preventing us from moving into a F.H.A. house had been worked through and we were given the go signal and a moving date. We would take possession of a seven room house on a beautiful tree lined street in St. Albans, Queens.

Having waited so long for this moment of triumph; I did not allow myself any spirited elation; but thanked God in my heart that he again had heard and answered my prayers. I did so long to live in a private house and even though we would be renting, it would be better than running up and down open stairwells and riding elevators. At long last Sam would have enough space to make a garden as large as he wished it to be. The house was attractively painted green and white, detached on both sides with a front and side entrance. Therefore we called it "The Green House." We moved into our new home on a rainy Easter Sunday. I was given four consecutive days off from work and for that, I was grateful; but I hated to use Easter Sunday for moving. I believed that it was raining that particular Easter Sunday because we were moving and not attending our Religious Services. Non-the-less we had Easter in our hearts and Valerie and Glen worked long and hard helping their father and the moving men get all our belongings into our new home. I realized it would take days before we would find all our belongings and find a place for everything, so I advised everyone to rest after all the initial moving was done. The first room that we all banded together to shape up was Valerie and Edie's room. It was a beautiful sunlit room with two large windows. I was contented once I knew my two girls had their furniture in place.

Over the next few weeks I went back and forth to work getting used to my nursing duties, learning something different every day. You see, what the actual work on a medical surgical floor is entirely different from what you are exposed to in a learning situation and just this subject alone would take quite a few chapters if I choose to reiterate. But what became uppermost in my mind at this time was the plight of Aunt Bertie. She seemed to be so "sacked in" and at home where she was at Marcus Garvey Nursing Home. She did not recognize me anymore as her niece but only as a nice lady who came to visit her from time to time. I knew that I could not help her alone in the house everyday because everyone was out during the daylight hours. Sam and I talked it over and it was decided that it would be feasible for her to stay at the Nursing Home since she seemed so comfortable and was receiving optional care.

One day Sam and I went to visit Aunt Bertie. Her nurse finally rolled her out to us in a wheelchair, fully dressed in a rose print dress, stockings and laced up black oxford shoes. She was the spitting image of my Mama and wore the same warm smile. If I did not know that my dear Mama was deceased some years earlier, I would have thought Aunt Bertie was she. The nurse turned her chair towards us.

"Here are your visitors," the nurse said. She gazed up at the both of us, a sunny smile creeping around her eyes. "You just landed?" was her inquiry. I looked at Sam nonplussed. God bless my husband, for he understood right away. "Yes he answered her without hesitation," "we just came in on the plane." "And we brought you something nice." He placed the little bag of fruit in her hands, opened it, took out a banana, peeled it half way down and placed it in her waiting hands. "Eat it slowly he said, you don't need to rush it down. She winked at him as she took a small bite. "You know Willie I always do as you say." She looked at his face and back to mine. Aunt Bertie now only saw two loving faces that locked her memory into by gone days. She had a mental block towards the present and the immediate past; wherein she had received such cruel treatment. She looked towards the open window where she could see the afternoon sun peeping through the curtains.

"Is it warm outside?" she asked. "Yes its spring going into summer" I replied. "Best time of year, "she sighed softly, her hand relaxing around the unfinished banana. Soon the Nurse came and took the bag of fruit out of her lap and said she would put the fruit in her fruit bowl on her bedside table. Looking at Aunt Bertie again I noticed sleep coming to her heavy eyelids. Will she ever be herself? I asked of Sam. He looked at me intently and explained. "She is more herself now, than what she has been for a long time." "You see, "he continued, her mind is back in her homeland of Bermuda with no cares or worries." She has not Rob to worry about and she honestly believes that I am her son Willie, visiting her. "Sam, dear Sam," I said, "you, have always been a son to my Auntie."

I awoke early one Saturday morning on my day off suddenly wondering to myself if at long last could there be a day in my life that is from mental stress.

Thank God I whispered, Thank you Jesus. All the Glory and the Praise belongs to you. How you have been with us through all our struggles and blunders. Sam Jr. was doing well in Parsons' College, having made the dean's list for the second time. Victor was out of the Navy given an honorable discharge because of those two big beautiful flat feet of his. Valerie having graduated from High School was attending Medgar Evers City University full time now. Glen was doing well in High School and expected to graduate with his class on time. Edie was a happy well-adjusted little girl whose only sin was to love everyone and to be so lovable herself. Sam was Dan's right hand man in the Garage Parking business. I was getting accustomed to the rigors and duties of the sick and suffering ever present in a hospital environment.

I looked over in my dresser mirror and pulled myself to sit upright in bed. Not bad for an old lady I mused, for someone is just past her middle forties. The Lord and I made good traveling companions I thought to myself, for we were on this journey together. Many were the time that I had no one to confide in but the Lord and he always proved faithful to me.

I tried to impart these feelings to Sam but he never seemed receptive to them He always felt that whatever a man's accomplishments were, good or bad were the direct results of his own efforts. But I could never deny the hand of God working in and through the weaving of our lives. All the good that resulted from our diligence, steadfastness, and honest endeavors, could never have been accomplished without the divine intertwining of the Holy Spirit of God in our lives and in our home. And when the dark days of despair and disappointment arose, as they so often did, I knew there was a lesson to be learned from these experiences, and still the Glory and the Praise belonged to God.

I hurriedly, showered, dressed and went down the hall steps of the Green House. It was a beautiful warm summer morning. Sam was out early in the morning before anyone else got up, digging in his garden. O how he loved his plants and shrubbery. Sometimes I felt he cared more for his gardens that he did for me. But I realized later when I pondered these thoughts over that they were only evil thoughts coming from the evil one and I did not further entertain these thoughts. Sam had never shown me any physical harm, only cold aloofness at times, which I attributed to his inner doubts and fears. He either talked too much to me and at me or remained silent and sullen for days. I tried to be a good listener whenever he wished to talk. I sensed a bitterness in his soul. I also gave this problem into the hands of the Lord and refused to allow it to blight my inner peace. In other words I adjusted my reactions to Sam's actions and went along with the flow. I know now at the time of this writing some twenty or more years later that this was the wrong course to follow. But I felt at that time and during that era that peace and harmony should be maintained at all cost.

He had just watered his flowers and grass and everything was glistening in the morning sun.

Several bird families were calling to each other as they flitted from tree to tree. A half dozen robin redbreasts were hopping about on the ground along with the sparrows. An occasional cardinal paid us a visit on that sparkling morning. I pointed the birds out to Sam. He stopped with hose in hand to notice. The blue jays were out another familiar group and always seen in pairs. A quiet aura rested over the scene as I stood in the doorway to the back yard garden. The fragrance from the lilacs and the roses hung in the air. I stepped down the few steps, turned around and looked back up at the windows of the Green House. Everything was peaceful and quiet. I endeavored to relish the moment.

Sam turned and said to me with a sweep of a gloved hand. "Do you like what we have here?" I nodded approval and sniffed at the air. "Come girl," he said, "lets leave everything and go get some breakfast." We jumped in the car and headed towards the Avenue, a new Fast Food store had just opened up. Sam always felt that when the moment was too heavy for words, that he should fill his mouth with food.

CHAPTER SEVENTEEN

Reach Out and Touch

There is one memory very vivid from my kindergarten days. Our teacher went around the circle of our tiny wooden chairs, pointing to each of us and asking, "Billy what do you want to be when you grow up?" "A Fireman" was Billy's reply. "And Sarah" she would continue, "What do you want to be?" "A Mommy," was her giggly reply, kicking her patent leathers in front of her. Each time the teacher would ask them they would always have different answers. The truth was now that I think about it, they themselves did not really know at such a young and tender age, what they wanted to be when they grew up. But somehow I knew what I wanted to be. I knew from a very early age I wanted to be a Nurse.

As a little girl, I liked to draw, write stories and read, read, read. But I always knew that I could not just "play" at being a Nurse, I had to be one. I must admit I was a little apprehensive during some of my earlier encounters with Hospital settings as a young child. The idea fascinated me and so intrigued me, that one could alter another's feelings of well being by touching and being near. As young children, Jeanie and I always played out childish games together. Jeanie always wanted to play "Bride and Groom." We had gone to a few weddings and had seen the Bride stepping down the wide steps of the Catholic church on 166th Street and Prospect Ave. Jeanie remembered how beautifully they were dressed in satin and lace. Mama had a rough dried clothes bag that she kept in the closet of her bedroom. In this bag were all kinds of curtains that needed to be dampened and ironed out, whenever Mama could get around to it. But Mama never seemed to find the time to iron out these white crinkly curtains and hang them up. These curtains were Jeanie's passion.

When Mama was busy in the washtub or making stew, Jeanie would say, lets play Bride and Groom. This meant draping the curtain material around her oval face, and using Mama's bobby pins, she would secure the material to her fat top braid. She would gaze at herself lovingly and smooth out the material down around her shoulders. My job was to pick up the bottom of the curtain veil and hum "Here comes the Bride." I never liked my part in this game of charades but I acquiesced because Jeanie had to be my patient when we played Nurse, and she did allow me to look in her ears and poke in her mouth.

I do believe Mama made it very convenient for Jeanie and I to play these games. I don't remember Mama ever smoothing out the lacy curtains tucked away in the rough dried laundry bag, in the bottom of her clothes closet.

I think to myself sometimes how Jeanie always wanted to be a Bride and how this experience eluded her. I thank God how my life long dream of becoming a Nurse was fulfilled. I made it against heavy odds. Sometimes the odds seemed greatly stacked against me. It was hard to leave my little Edie everyday and go off to nursing school. She at first was such a lonely little girl born after her other siblings were growing up and almost out of her reach. The burden of her care and some of the household chores were shared between Valerie and Glen. This saddened me sometimes because I felt I was curtailing their youthful activities. But thank God they understood what God had imparted to them and they fully cooperated. Sam was fearful for our future and rightfully so. It was very hard for any woman back in that era of time to take some kind of training, or education to better herself. The Phrase "Women's Rights" was now being bandied about. I did not fully understand the implications of this movement and really didn't think much about it. My only aim was to become a good Nurse to satisfy my deep longings to help, care for the suffering and to try to make a difference among the poor community, as I knew it to be then. Nursing was my spiritual calling. I knew I could serve God willingly and faithfully in this capacity. I was happy and contented when working on my hospital floor. It was a challenge. The work was taxing and brain boggling. Nursing not ever was, or is it now the way it is depicted on television. It is very grueling and heart rendering, and especially so if you function correctly. The Nurse is the middleman. The nurse is the fall guy. They must be able to interact between the doctor and the patient; between administration and the patient; and between the patient, the Community and the environment. And if the Nurse is not able to carry out the many demands and functions, someone invariably will be hurt, injured or become unsalvageable.

When the graduate nurse walks down the aisle of the hospital auditorium, holding the lit lamp in the palms of their two hands taking the Nursing oath, they are telling the world that the care of the sick and suffering are being put above the nurse's own needs. The impact of the oath might not be readily evident, but only in a few days, it will be realized the true impact of the oath.

Yes the nurse punches a time clock in and out. For pay purposes only, but their time is not their own. She is expected on her hospital floor and at her station at least ten minutes before due time. She must listen to the report on the patients, get her assignment and assess her patients. She must make rounds with the doctors and assist the doctors with their treatments. Nursing is a continuing twenty-four hour job. The Nurse cannot shut the doors of her brain when punching out to go home. She will remember the open bloody wounds, the cries and groans of the painfully tormented, and the loud blinking signal lights of the finished intravenous solution bottles, long after her drowsy eyes close in sleep.

And there is much to learn and everyday something new to remember. Interaction with the Doctors and all health care workers is most important. What was studied and learned in Nursing School now comes to a full circle. I believe it is in the first year of actual Nursing on an acute care floor that you put to practice all the "Stuff" that you learned, and the "stuff" is the reasons for your actions.

It took me about a full year as expected to recover myself and to be able to look at myself in the mirror and be satisfied that I was beginning to work out. A Nurse will never ever fully arrive. If she thinks so, then she becomes stagnant. There is so much to learn everyday. She must read and read every periodical and notable events pertaining to her specific job. She must be aware of new systems and procedures. Although now out of the classroom, she must attend classes and seminars when appointed to and the opportunity presents itself. She must be able to report immediately to her subordinates, her peers and supervisors with clarity and accuracy.

She must be clean and immaculate at all times with spotless white uniforms and a crisp white cap and your Nursing School pin in sight on your collar. This was the dress code of my day. I know now as I am writing this that Nurses have wider options and different dress codes but it is not the uniform that counts, but what and who is wearing the uniform and how they function.

When I graduated from Nursing School my passion as I thought then, was to be a Pediatric Nurse. But I was advised that I needed experience on an acute care Medical Surgical floor. So I was thrown out in this arena. I said thrown out because I really had no choice in the matter. The institution where I took my training, needed new fresh talent as they said, and after being so trained, were not willing to give us up to any other category but the most needful at that time, which was the "One Step

Down", Medical Surgical acute care floor.

We had a small six-bedded General I.C.U. unit on this "Ill reputed," (as we called it) nursing floor. The I.C.U. dept. was in the middle of the floor across from the elevator. We had forty one other beds with very sick patients in closer range to the Nursing Station. Four isolation rooms were maintained at the end of the corridor, four rooms at each end, counting eight isolation units in all, maintained on this acute care Medical Surgical floor. These patients were isolated mainly for tuberculosis, Hepatitis and often times for reverse isolation. This was the case when the patient had to be protected, from other germs and bacteria that he or she in their debilitated state could not fight off themselves.

These isolated patients were usually very sick and weak with intravenous solutions in progress to receive medication such as blood thinners, antibiotics and hyper alimentation therapy that is nutrition through the veins.

I was a Licensed Practical Nurse. Upon my graduation, I was admonished about my certain functions. But in a short period of time I learned there was a very thin line between the "RN" nurse and the L.P.N. nurse. We were identified as such by our I.D. tags, nursing school pins, Nursing Caps and paychecks. In the institution where I worked, the L.P.N. took part in all emergencies, codes, worked in the I.C.U., gave medicine, injections, hung blood, and even in the first two years of my experience we were expected to mix a highly sterile hyper alimentation solution in our closed medication room, wearing gloves, masks, and cover gowns. The code cart had to be checked everyday by the L.P.N., making sure that all emergency drugs were on the cart, and up to date and all electrical systems in good working condition. We were responsible for the keys to the locked controlled drugs and for ordering and picking up such drugs from the pharmacy. Therefore we were finger printed, and so responsible for such heavy-duty drugs as narcotics and barbiturates also methadone.

I loved my job when I was working. I loved the interaction with the other Health Care givers. There was never a dull moment. I was always on my toes, but when all this sweat and action was transpiring, I would function as a robot, attacking each job and assignment instinctively. But on my "Days Off', would come the sighs of relief. And yes, there was always a satisfying feeling. A satisfied feeling of knowing a job was well done. It took only a soft hand on my arm, a weak smile when the pain relieved, a hug from a family member when reassured; and this was my satisfying portion, and thanks enough indeed.

The days came and went quickly. Oh! those were the most memorable days. I think back on them with mixed emotions. I remember when the assignments were so tedious and the medications so heavy with never ending new orders that had to be picked up and transferred to our little medication tickets that we were responsible for. Those were the days when the Nurse had to travel about from room to room with those precious medication tickets in her already bulging pockets or on her medication tray. Usually she was responsible for about twenty to thirty tickets in a given day or eight hour tour. And one of the most unforgivable sins that a Nurse could commit at this time, aside from making poor judgment, was to carry these tickets home with her in her uniform pocket, which all of us did do at one time or the other. This was a very unforgivable act because it meant the oncoming Nurse, had to not only check out the Doctors orders which is what she was required to do anyway, but she had to write out the tickets corresponding. These were the days before the one medication truck was manned by one Nurse at a time for a specific unit. The one "Medication Truck" was a new revolution in Nursing and made medicating the Patients a much easier chore. Each patient had his or her own medication drawer and the medicine came up from the Pharmacy already measured and labeled.

We had to know our medications, its actions, and side effects. There was never any room for error, and such a sin was inexcusable, and if such did occur, three days of suspension was in order and a hearing with the Union Representative and your Nursing Supervisor. In those days there were very few medication errors, because the Nurse read the Doctors' orders herself and used the patients chart to check and double check. The next unforgivable sin was the sin of a tired nurse, a nurse who was not aware of fatigue. That a seven to eight day work week could be done in succession with sometimes only two days off. Back then in the institution where I worked, the nurses had to work two weekends before getting one weekend off. We never knew how tired we were until the schedule was completed. Nevertheless, God was always good to me. I never forgot the time when each of us had what it seemed like such impossible assignments. Patients were very ill. We had very limited supplies and we had to attend constant meetings. At this time, back in 1975, we had an ex-army nurse for a supervisor. She had forgotten that she was no longer in the Army shouting orders to her kaki-uniformed nurses overseas. We the nurses looked at each other in dismay as she stormed in and out of patient's rooms, with flying papers behind her, giving commands.

We gathered about the Nursing station desk one morning when she was on one of her rampages. I never will forget the scene; it was five of us not counting the Head

Nurse. Having listened to the report and received our assignments, we knew we were in for a bad day. We had three patients on blood therapy and six Isolation patients. Four on the D.L. (danger list) needing total care. We had one Circo-Electric Bed patient with decubiti (meaning bed sores) the size of cut watermelons needing two nurses in attendance. Also, many were on intravenous therapy. We gathered close together and spontaneously held hands. We bowed our head and a quiet prayer escaped my lips. I had not planned to pray at this time although I had thought about it many times. How we did need divine guidance. I felt this particular morning that I needed supernatural help, help from the Lord above to give us grace and stamina to perform our tasks that day. I did not say any long drawn out prayer. It was very simple and straight from the heart. When the prayer was over, we each said a quiet Amen. There standing behind us was our Army Nurse as we sometimes called her with hands on her hips and her eyes narrowing. She did not dare to utter a word. I believe we gained her respect that day. She then had no choice but to realize that she no longer had the last word on the fourth floor of that Hospital Institution. Our help came from another source. From the Lord God Almighty from Jesus Christ my personal Savior. I don't know just how many of our staff knew my Savior personally, but I do know that they knew for sure that we were in need of his help from day to day to be our guide in carrying out our Nursing duties. This little epistle is not meant to be any disrespect to our supervisors and those in command, because surely we understood that every working situation must be orderly.

From then on, dear Nurse in mention was not only aware of our compensations, but also of our capacities and subsequently reciprocated with concern and respect.

God is Good! His mercy endureth forever. If it were not for God's mercies, I would not have been able to endure the rigors of nursing on such an acute care floor for nineteen years. As a young woman starting out, I was so inhibited and introverted never welcoming an argument or involved in any controversy of any kind. I was always willing to go along with the flow, maintaining peace at all cost. This was not the way of the outside world. Everyday was a new challenge, and the Nurse was the patient's advocate, his first line of defense.

The Patients emotional, physical and spiritual needs had to be addressed, and safe guarded everyday. My greatest and most memorable reward in every case was when the patient recovered and was able to say Goodbye and go home in reasonable optional health.

CHAPTER EIGHTTEEN

Watch Ye Therefore
While Praying

Some of my retirement time was spent outdoors, early in the morning, walking briskly and numbering the blocks when I walked here in Brooklyn with the idea in mind that the exercise would help to keep me fit. I would greet people along the way, always marveling to myself, how the folks in Brooklyn were so friendly. I would walk past the Nursing Home across from the building where I lived and greet the residents there. They would be sitting on the outside benches, rocking, with listless eyes and some rolling around in their wheelchairs. They were a pitiful lot some too sick or handicapped to go home and be alone.

I became friendly with a little wrinkled faced lady who would watch and waited for me around 9:30 AM on Friday mornings. She knew this was my shopping day, and I would pass by the gate on my way home from the store. She never took any of the fruit I offered her; she only wanted me to pause, leaning on my shopping cart and listen to her stories of the Good old days. She said she would soon be eighty years old, but I am not sure if she knew just how far into eighty years, for she told me stories that I heard my parents speak about. Sometimes I would walk down in the opposite direction and come back by a different route. But I would always be marching and singing hymns, so that my body would not forget that my daily walks was a form of exercise.

But one morning I think, I almost became a statistic for I fell among thieves. There was no Good Samaritan passing by, no knowing friendly neighbor close at hand; I was only covered by the Blood of Jesus. I will never, ever, forget this incident; it will always be fresh in my mind everyday, because it is a miracle that I came out of this experience unscathed.

I had been to the store, and coming from a different direction, carrying a red canvas bags with my groceries. I had bought a loaf of bread, a quart of milk, some chicken wings and a few other small items. I was holding my football bag as I used to call it, clutched tightly under my left arm. I noticed a lady crossing the avenue up ahead of me and coming directly towards me. I noticed her so intently because she resembled one of my cousins. The same hairdo and build, but as she approached me I saw that she was a much younger person.

As she came closer, she paused, and then dashed over to the grassy lawn in front of the houses that I was passing and made a loud outcry.

"Oh goodness! look what I found." She darted back and directly in front of me, pushing a fat shiny wallet in front of me.

"It says District 29 Lady, Where is District 29?" I replied "I don't know Miss," and tried to move out of her pathway.

"Look lady! Look Lady, look what's here." She was very insistent as she opened the wallet and flipped through wads and wads of green bills. It was new crisp money, with more zeroes behind the numbers that I have eyes on my face. I could not believe what I was seeing and my mouth flew open; for I had never seen that amount of money all at one time in no time of my life.

"I know nothing about this lady, and I want nothing to do with it," I was saying as I tried to move away, but she was in front of me again.

"You saw this lady," she said. "I did not steal it" "You saw me pick it up over there" pointing to the grassy spot between the iron railings.

"Look lady," she insisted, "Its at least one hundred and fifty thousand dollars, and you saw me pick it up. "This is an answer to prayers," she cried out throwing her head back and lifting her eyes up to the sky. "I asked God for a blessing," oh yes I did," she continued, "Thank you Jesus, this is my blessing." "Lady" she eyed me with beady eyes, don't you believe in answered prayer?" She was getting me now, "Yes I murmured slowly eyeing the stacked green bills in a black worn out wallet.

I know now, that at this point, I should have been aware, alert to the whiles of the devil. God does not bless his children with apprehension and uncertainty, and surely I knew then that if this was a blessing, it was a blind one, because I did not see it as one.

As she stood in front of me talking, a tall well dressed black man came across the same Avenue that she did, walking fast past us as if to pass us by, she called out to him. "Sir, Sir, excuse me, do you know where District 29 is?" "No, Miss, he answered, "I don't live around here, I'm just coming from my lawyers office." He whipped out a folded white handkerchief and wiped around his forehead. "I have business up the street and I'm already late," he said as he glanced at his watch.

"Please Sir, the woman said apologetically, look at what I just found." He paused again to look at his watch. "Well" he said, what's this all about?"

"This is found money, Sir, and this lady saw me pick it up over there." he held her hand holding the billfold with pretended wide eyes of surprise.

"Good Lord! Its money all right, but is it counterfeit or the real stuff?" His fingers flipped through the bills "How much you think?" he asked the woman. "Don't know, at least one hundred and fifty thousand dollars, she said. "We got to go somewhere and count it."

"I don't think so," I replied. "I'm not going anywhere to count anything", I said. She looked at me again through squinting eyelids. "What's the matter with you," she said. "Don't you need money?" "Don't you pray for a blessing?" The word pray, lit up my mind. "I pray all the time," I whispered to myself. I knew one of my sons, was house hunting, how I could really help him, I thought to myself. This would be a little financial boost for him.

"My car is just across the street," the well dressed black man said between even white teeth. "My nephew is out here with me, He's at the wheel." "Come let's go," he said. "We can count it out and divide it up in the car." I pulled back, hesitant, this was happening too fast. "No! No! I said I don't think this is kosher. This was always the word I used when I wasn't sure of the validity of any situation.

"Come Mother, the man said." "Let me carry your bag." "You look tired," and before I knew what was happening, he was ahead of me with my red canvas shopping bag, that Valerie had given me that same Mother's Day of that year. The woman had me by the arm, guiding me across the street, whispering in my ear, "just thank Jesus, that's all." "Don't throw His blessing back in His face. It was after 10AM now, I could tell by the height of the sun. I worried now, that the children would soon be calling me, as they did every day to see that I was back in the house, after my morning walk or shopping spree. My two daughters especially called me every morning. They worried if I was out after noon, because as they would say, "Its two dangerous to walk the streets of Brooklyn, alone after noon. I usually listened to them because I did not want them to worry about me. I had done enough worrying about each of my children for different reasons. That was what parents were supposed to do, care for and worry over their children, not the other way around.

The tall black man had already gotten across the street ahead of us, toting my red shopping bag and his skinny black brief case. The cars were whizzing by us. It seemed as if the woman and I were dodging traffic in order to catch up to the man who was on his way up the street. He stopped in front of an ugly battered silver car with a black vinyl top. He was speaking hurriedly to someone at the wheel. The woman was pulling me on, yet telling me in a now suspicious cajoling voice "you're going to be thanking God, for this day, Mother." "Don't worry she continued, everything is going to turn for your good, from now on, because you're a child of God." These words kind of calmed my spirit, but I know now I should have been more alert to the wiles of the devil. I know now that everyone that names the name of Jesus is not always a true Christian. But at this point I must confess I was not a watchful Christian. Watchfulness means as I am certain of now, always being alert to what's going on about you. These two, the woman and the man helped me into the front seat of this raggedy old 1970 model. In the driver's seat was this skinny malnutrition looking youth of maybe twenty years old. The tall black man introduced him, "This is my nephew Cleo." "He's a quiet fellow," he continued, He doesn't mean any harm to anyone." "I'm glad I brought him along."

The young man hunched his shoulders, licked his lips and didn't utter a sound. The woman broke in quickly, "Lets count this stuff." "There are a lot of green backs here." "At least one hundred and fifty thousand dollars in large bills." "Oh look," she called out. "Look what's here!" "A note of instructions". "It says, Jack take care of this for us. I've been to the race track, and I'm going back again in two weeks time." She continued on reading, "say nothing to Marvin." "I'll see you in Florida, I'll tell you when." "Oh Lord the skinny man said those bills are marked. We should turn the whole thing in." A light turned on in my head. I'm in the soup for sure now, I whispered under my breath.

"What's that she asked grabbing the shoulder pad in my jacket. I had worn a jacket that bright sunny September morning. September 28th on a Monday morning to be exact. Every time I see that jacket hanging in my closet, I am thankful for those big bulking shoulder pads that we ladies were wearing in all our clothes. I noticed her nails as she clutched at my jacket. They were long and red like devils claws. She repeated herself. "You say something Mother."

I turned now, and looked her straight in the face "What's your name?" I asked, "I don't even know your name." She laughed out loud and grabbed at my shoulder again. "My name dearie is Ubenia Johnson." Its spelled just like it sounds. UBENIA." "Some handle isn't it," she went on giggling to herself. I think Moms was mad at Pops at the time.

The man now interjected. "And I'm Mr. Hayes," and today is my very lucky day, because I just made a settlement with my lawyer up the street for five thousand dollars." I had a little accident, a very convenient one, not so long ago." He laughed loudly slapping her knee. A chill slipped down and across my back. These two knew each other. This is a hoax, a scam, and I'm not in the soup, I'm in a stew.

"Now tell us what's your name, Mother," he continued. We cannot divide the money until we know each other. "My name is Mrs. Samuels, I replied." "I'm Mrs. Charles Samuels. Using my husband's first name, and my father's first name. You still use your husband's first name, the man asked in surprise. Yes I do, I said emphatically trying not to sound bold. "Yes I do use his name as long as he pays the bills."

"Well I'll be switched he said in astonishment. " I shuttered, my teeth felt cold. I don't remember praying. I remember saying, "No! No! I don't think this is any good; I got to get home to my house. My children will be calling me. "And when you do get home you'll be loaded," the man snorted under his breath. He took out the same folded hankie, snapped it open this time and proceeded to blow out his nasal passages with loud honking noises.

The young man sitting in front at the wheel was motionless. He did not join in at all in the back and forth conversation. In fact he seemed put upon not included in the scheme. The woman Ubenia became very serious at this point. "How do we know these bills are not counterfeit," she said. I'll have to go up the street to "The Job" and run them through the machine." If the green light stays on, then they are OK! "If the red light comes on, then they are no good!" I hope Mark is there, she continued. "If he is there, then he'll check the serial numbers also. "You know," she said, he's the money man in this neighborhood." "He owns all these little shops and stores out here in Brooklyn in this neighborhood. "Yes sir! She continued, he's the moneyman for real. Everyone knows Mark, but they don't know who he really is.

She put her hand on the door handle and was out the door in a split second with the wallet of money in her hand.

I closed my eyes now and thought to myself, how could this be happening to me? I prayed everyday for divine protection and guidance, and here I am now stuck in a situation that snagged me so quickly and unexpectedly. I was not watchful. I was caught off guard. My praying spirit came alive now. "Lord! Lord! I cried out in my heart. Cover me right now, with thy precious blood. I don't know how to get out of this, or what move to make. I looked up and down the street where we were parked to see if I could make a quick escape. My red canvas bag filled with my groceries was resting on his shoes. I said quickly, ""Give me my bag please." He put a heavy restraining hand on my shoulder. "Everything is going to be alright," he said. She'll be back soon, and we'll know for sure if the bills are legit. I gave a deep sigh, placed my head in my hands and prayed silently. She said she would be back in no time. The "no time" seemed endless hours. Soon the woman with the ugliest name of Ubenia came hurriedly around the corner raising a fist in victory as she came towards the car. She laughed as she got in the car. "The bills are all good, everyone of them." "The green light stayed on and Mark recorded the serial numbers." "There's fifty thousand for each of us she rattled on in animation.

My mind was clouding over now. Is this real? Something is wrong. This is all wrong and I'm caught up in it. She crooned on, "Oh course you know, we'll give our driver a hundred dollars, each one of us. She's the master mind I said to myself, Lord help me to get out of this one in one piece.

"And just one more thing," she said quietly, and slowly, "It's going to cost each one of us a little something." "Understand?" she continued. "How much?" the skinny black man called out as if answering his cue. "Not much," she said, "not much when you consider what you're getting. You're each getting fifty thousand dollars, and Mark wants twelve hundred from each of us. I opened my mouth when I should have remained quiet. "Deduct it then from each share." I said. "That's what the woman wanted. She wanted me to show interest, and now she had the upper hand.

"No Deary, we can't do that because he recorded the serial numbers and broke the bills up for us." She was talking fast now, you know you cannot put that large amounts of money in your account without declaring your business." I was really confused now.

"Something's not right," I said, "I feel it in my bones. She gave me a sour look and smirked at me, "Maybe your bones." She gave me a sour look and smirked at me, "maybe your bones are too old to believe in answered prayer.

She continued on, now really, clutching the shoulder of my jacket. "Do you have a couple of diamonds or emeralds, some valuable jewelry maybe?" I was apprehensive now. I only wanted to get out of this predicament alive. "I have nothing" I said, nothing at all." "No cash? She asked. How do you pay your bills? My husband writes out checks every month." "I don't want anything to do with this scheme."

"OK! OK!" she said, we can't force her. Lets take her to Aunties house. "She'll take your place, and you'll sign a note releasing your share to her, and you'll owe no one anything, OK? "Okay; lets go."

I heard myself mouthing the words. "Let me out here." "No Mother, the woman answered, "we're going to Aunties house, so there won't be any comeback from you." I blurted out, "What's my part in this?" "Now that's more like it," said the woman. "And there won't be any comeback from you." "What bank do you do your business?" I whispered it under my breath. But they seemed to know the answer. It dawned on me, that they might have seen me in my bank or leaving it at some time or other. In other words, I must have been trailed. She definitely was the master mind, and I knew now that the three of them knew each other.

We had begun to drive around, not to Aunties house anymore as she said, "to this young ladies bank." She was trying to perk me up by referring to me as young lady, but I knew what I was up against and I thought within myself; when I get to the bank I'll make a run for it. She surely was the commander and chief of the whole operation. "Here we are," she soon said to the driver. He knew just which Bank branch to go to without directions "Find a parking space as close as you can." I placed my hand on the rusty door handle and thought about quickly jumping out on my side, which was curbside. "Help Mother out," she said to the young man, and hold onto her, don't let her get hurt."

There was no line, no waiting. I always carried my bank card in my wallet in my purse. I looked about. Everybody was doing his or her own business. I saw no guard, and if I did what could I do with the young man so close at my elbow. So I wrote up my slip for twelve hundred dollars and watched while the teller counted it over to me. Deep sorrow filled my heart at that moment; not for the loss of the money but because I had not been watchful and careful, that I allowed myself to fall into this terrible trap which is the wiles of the devil. The tall lanky youth guided me across the street with a firm hand on my arm and helped me back into the front seat of the car. The woman quickly put out her hand to me. "Let me count it," she said. She paused soon. "It's all here, now lets find Mark." He has your share and this is his for processing your money. You'll get it all broken down in fives, tens, twenty's and fifties." "That'll be some bundle," she said. He'll have it all wrapped up for you, and this is his," she continued waving my twelve hundred dollars at me.

Then we drove a good distance away from the bank. We seemed to be driving around in circles. I saw no police officer, or patrol car. I was not sure what I would do if I did see the police.

Soon we stopped on a quiet street with a vacant lot at the end of the block. The woman got out the car. I'll be right back she said to the driver. He was staring out the window and made no answer whatsoever. She walked briskly up the block looking behind her. In less than five minutes she was back again. She came towards the car and beckoned me to get out. No one got out with me. No one was on the street, and I felt chilly and alone. I noticed the woman was carrying a small flat purse, which I did not remember seeing before. Did she have a gun on her, or in her purse I worried to myself. The air was chilly now, and the almost noonday sun had hidden behind some clouds. I looked to the end of the vacant lot, where two mangy dogs were sniffing at the ground.

She pointed up the street. "Mark is up the street in the Laundry Mat on this side of the street," she said matter-of-factly. He is waiting for you. He is wearing a wide brimmed black hat. I hesitated looking at her and up the street. She said again, "Hurry up, he's waiting for you with your money. I turned and watched her get back into the car. I clutched my bag, which I had not ever put down, closer under my arm, and hurried up the street looking for the Laundry Mat and the Man Mark with the wide brimmed black hat. The man who supposedly owned all the little shops and stores in the neighborhood. There were just a few stragglers now on the broken steps as I passed the shabby houses. I was at the end of the block now. There was only a candy store and a smoke shop but no Laundry Mat. Two women looked at me questioningly. They knew, I was unfamiliar in the neighborhood. I said nothing, felt nothing, only clear cold stark realization that there was no Laundry Mat, no Mark, no fifty thousand dollars and I was twelve hundred dollars the poorer. I turned and started to go back to the car, but as I walked on, I realized there was no car waiting for me. Why should there be? This was all a scam, a hoax quickly pulled off when my guard was down. I groaned as I walked on. What was the lesson? My soul be on thy guard at all times, waking or sleeping, and especially while praying. "Oh dear God I cried to myself." My heart was a hard knot inside my chest. I had disappointed my Lord and Savior. I had fallen to the wiles of the devil. I had not been watchful. I was not aware of the trickery of the present world.

I was a good distant from home, but I walked it pondering to myself. Should I call the police? Give a description? My children would be appalled at the fact that I allowed myself to fall prey to such scammers, to fall into such a trap. I could not tell anyone, I was so ashamed; to think I had allowed myself to be coerced into a scheme. For days I hated myself. It was on my mind every waking hour, but I could not bring myself to speak about it to anyone.

It has been over a year now since this happened to me. My soul was more injured than any physical injury that I have ever experienced on my person. I found myself soon after this episode, praying more earnestly and reading my Bible for longer periods. Not just grabbing a few bible verses to carry me through the day, but digging deeper in the scriptures, and feeding on God's word. I saw in some of those precious versus, "Vengeance is Mine, I will repay saith the Lord." I used to think to myself. "I have no enemies." "Everyone is so kind to me." Everyone respects my person. Being a Senior Citizen, I learned my lesson the hard and cruel way. Put not your trust in man. I also understood the Divine protection of God. He was in control during the whole time of this incidence. He did not allow me to panic, and they could do me no bodily harm.

As the days came and went, I began to feel the loving divine care of my Savior. I became more aware of the dreadful things going on in our neighborhood, our cities, and country and all because the people had turned from the True and Living God. Come back! Come back America and turn again to the True and Living God.

CHAPTER NINETEEN

Till the Shadow Flee Away

I had reached my sixty-second birthday. I was tired, weary, worn out and it was time for me to say goodbye. Saying goodbye to eighteen years of Nursing was not easy. I had learned a lot during this time in my life. Not only medical perceptions, but also how to be human, caring and honest. I learned in my first classes of nursing theory, that a good Nurse must use his or her head, heart and hands. I was satisfied that I had fulfilled my early dreams of becoming a good Nurse. Having kept my home and raised my children, I felt it was time now for me to hang up my "Star of David" Nursing cap, put aside my homemaking gadgets and take long walks and smell the flowers along the way.

Well, thanks be to God, He allowed me these pleasures for three years. I shopped, cooked special dishes when I wanted to and served my family. I visited the Library and read all kinds of books at leisure. These were my fun days, I was carefree and footloose. I loved my church, The Bethel Gospel Tabernacle in Queens and worshipped as often as I could with my family. I got to know my young Grandson Glenny Jr. and we got to be good buddies. I did not know that there were shadows waiting for me just up the road around the bend, where the beautiful flowers grew. I had no precise symptoms of my impending illness. I made my sixty fifth birthday on January 4th, 1993. I went to church the Sunday before the fourth with my eldest son Sam Jr. and visited my husband Sam Sr. at his residence. My husband Sam was at this time a post stroke patient, wheelchair bound, but able to manage with a homemaker. We had been separated for many years at this time, but there was no animosity between us, and since we were not living together under the same roof, we had become true friends. Our hearts were intertwined with the memories of our early marriage and the rearing of our family. We had a pleasant visit that day and Sam showed me his progress in the use of the walker. Coming home I was pleasantly tired and went to bed early.

The next day after my birthday was an uneventful day. I arose early, went to the bank and took care of some business. I ate a light lunch and piddled around my little apartment; I called it piddling when doing none specific things. Towards evening, I felt a shadow across my left eye. It felt as though I had a piece of hair or web in my eye. When Edie, my youngest daughter called to ask about my welfare, as she always did, I related to her that I thought I had something foreign in my left eye. She brought me home some eye drops from the Drugstore.

The next morning I woke up fresh as a daisy as I thought. I said my prayers, read my Bible and was ready for the day. I had loads of laundry ready to be tackled. But I felt a little lazy as the morning wore on, so I decided to do a little cooking and catch up on my reading. That night, I awoke with a terrific pounding headache. It was high over the center of my eyes. It was a strong pounding headache. I took some medicine and it was relieved after a longer period than usual. When daylight dawned, I knew there was something definitely wrong with me because I could not see the words in my Bible. I did not tell my daughters, Edie or Valerie at this time because I knew they would worry, and I thought I needed my glasses changed. But as the afternoon drew on, the shadows began to fall. I did not dream that I would be writing a chapter such as this one in my Tapestries. But as I said in my earlier writings, there are all different colored threads that make for a beautiful design in a Tapestry. Usually the underside of the tapestry is ugly, crudely done, and indistinguishable, but when the piece is finished, then the right side of the design is beautiful and the motif is clear.

By the end of the week of January 9th, 1993, I was in the hospital diagnosed by the medical & surgical doctors and a reputable neurologist as having a brain aneurism and an adenoma on the pituitary gland, sometimes called the Master gland. This gland rightly called so because it governs the activity of body functions metabolism and the functions of other endocrine glands. It is a small oval shaped body hanging by a stem under the base of the brain in the frontal area of the skull.

I learned all about the pituitary gland in Nursing School. It was the boss over the other glands in the body. What I suddenly became aware of was the fact that if the Pituitary gland became ill or incompatible it could not give direction to the other glands which depended on it to do so. I became very much aware of my Pituitary gland. It was no longer a page in my Taber's Encyclopedia or my Nursing Textbooks, but a little buddy of mine. I called it a "her", my little Petty Terrie. She was holding onto a very heavy load, the size of a green olive and it was making her tired and sick. As a result of her fatigue, the adenoma was resting on my optic nerve, which was causing a stealthy blindness. If this were not corrected soon there would be progressive deepening shadows. My doctors wanted to intervene soon, without delay. I opted to go home and pray about the situation and to talk to my spiritual guide, The Bishop in our church.

I had two doctors who were attending me at the time. There were two very serious surgical procedures that needed to be done almost immediately if my sight was to improve at all. One was a craniotomy and the clipping off of the aneurism and drainage of the blood vessel to prevent hemorrhage in the brain. The other procedure was a resection of the adenoma, growing on the pituitary gland. It was obvious that the craniotomy had to be done first. So thus I understood the need for these two very serious operations in those early days of the new year of 1993.

Well, I talked to my dear Bishop Sr. over the telephone. He was up in his ninety years and unable to travel about, but he prayed for me over the telephone, very reassuring prayers of faith and encouragement. The children and I decided there was nothing else I could do but to stretch out on God's unchanging promises and place myself in the Hospital of both of the Doctors' choice. Thus I was admitted for the first surgical procedure which was a craniotomy. The first of February found me in the recovery room swathed in head bandages and a catheter attached draining small amounts of excess blood from the operative site. I do not know how, when the surgery commenced in the O.R. that early Thursday morning around 7:30 A.M. I was knocked out but locked in the arms of Jesus as the deft fingers of the Neuro surgeon removed part of my skull and performed a very delicate operation on my brain. God is the one who guided those skillful fingers of that very talented young man. I praise God for his intelligence because the Bible states that all perfect and good gifts come down from the Father above, where there is no variableness or shadow of changing.

I was placed in the Intensive Care Unit of the Neurology Dept of this Reputable Medical Institution in Brooklyn; where the personnel, Doctors and Nurses were specifically trained to care for such neurology patients as myself. I regained consciousness almost immediately, and began to show quick progress in recuperating.

I did not regain my sight at this time, for everything was still in shadows. I trusted my Savior Jesus Christ that the finished work was waiting for me around the corner.

For weeks the shadows remained. Everyone was a gray silhouette moving about with only his or her rings, earrings, or keys very evident to me. I learned to recognize my visitors by the shapes of their shadows and by whatever metals that had on their person. But I was not dismayed by this phenomenon. I trusted God knowing I was completely in his hands.

The second surgical procedure was scheduled for another two or three months after the first one. I was sent home on a heavy regime of medication to rest and recuperate. When I returned to my Doctors for follow-up care, they were very satisfied with my progress, and a date was set for the second surgical procedure.

My Bishop prayed again for me over the telephone. One of the Assistant Pastors visited me in the Hospital. Friends and family sent up special prayers for me because they realized I was going through a great test of affliction; but God had given me a child like faith. The doctor who was going to do the second procedure counseled us in his office and visited me in another hospital, which was a specialty Institution for these kinds of cases.

Here in this Special Hospital, I was visited by a barrage of doctors from several different departments. So many tests were taken. I had two MRI's one CAT scan and an angiogram. I was visited by a cardiologist, and Endocrinologist an ENT specialist and his assistants. Many blood tests were taken and at this point. I was beginning to feel like a pincushion. I was transported back and forth to other departments for eye exams and routine X-rays, all in preparation for the second operation. On the appointed day I was prepared and taken in the holding room of the Surgical Suite. Jesus Christ my Savior was waiting there for me. He knew I was coming and He had an appointment with my doctors. He communed with my Doctors and He allowed them to commence with the surgery guiding their expertise every step of the way.

Oh! Praise the Lord God Almighty, maker of the Universe. The one who flung the Sun, Moon and Stars in place was familiar with little insignificant me. He took charge of that whole situation in the O.R.

My doctors were prepared to remove and Adenoma from the pituitary gland which hung under the base of my brain, by going up under my nasal orifice. I do not know when the Adenoma, which is a tumor became an abscess which collapsed into fluid when touched by the surgeons' knife. The surgery took another turn, not for the worst but for the unexpected. Infectious fluids were now pouring through my whole system. But Thank God there was no tumor. My whole sinus mucosa had to be cleaned out for there was a gross bacterial infection enclosed in the abscess, which was found, attached to the pituitary gland. I came down from the O.R. with both of my nares packed with medical gauze, and I was only able to breathe from my mouth for five days. I was immediately infused with large doses of antibiotics to fight the infection seeping through my system during the operation. I was placed in the ICU unit. I was unable to breathe from my nose, surrounded by shadowy figures, moving quickly to and fro eager to keep me comfortable and to stabilize me and record my process.

I felt engulfed in The Holy Spirit of God. I was surrounded by His love and care. Everyone seemed as though they were ordained especially to nurse me. Kind loving hands cared for me. They washed me, changed me monitored my vital signs unrelentingly. After the next five days, the packing was removed from my nose. I then really began to feel better. My olfactory senses returned to me. Everything was a new wonder. The linen on my bed smelled so refreshing. I was also learning how to swallow all over again because with the packing in both my nares I was afraid to swallow for fear of choking. I enjoyed a cold slice of watermelon as never before. My first sneeze after surgery was a marvel to me.

Doctors from far and near came to visit me. They flashed lights in my eyes and up in my nose. I heard such remarks as "Looks good," "Healing nicely." What I did not realize right off, was that a piece of fatty tissue was removed from my left lower abdomen which they had to place somewhere up under my brain to "wall off" as they called it the brain from the mucosa sinus cavity. I was advised not to blow my nose for four weeks, to watch for bleeding from my nose and if any to report it right away to my nurses and care givers.

I finally was allowed to walk to the bathroom. I was very weak and unsteady at first and needed assistance for the short trip from my bed to the bathroom. But one morning as I went to the bathroom on the arm of one of my nurse, the black toilet seat rose up to meet me. The small bathroom was dimly lit but I saw the black contrast of the toilet seat against the white walls. Thank God my eyesight was returning. I was beginning to see objects much clearer now.

The doctors and Hospital personnel were astounded at my progress. They planned to move me soon from the critical care unit to the One Step Down Neurology Care floor. This move was expedited with the help of my sons, moving my bed and tables and the personal items that I had accumulated in the days I spent in that critical care unit. I was moved into another room with two beds. A patient who had a very serious back problem occupied the bed by the window. She seemed to be very limited in her mobility. Unable to walk at all, she was transferred with assistance from the Nurses in and out of her wheelchair. She was maintained with pelvic traction when not in the wheelchair. This lady seemed to be in constant pain and misery, and to my dismay, after listening to her complaints; I realized her problems were not only physical but also emotional and spiritual. Her name was Myra Dugan, a young lady in her mid forties.

The days followed one another in rapid succession. I had an intravenous infusion going in my left arm. I was receiving antibiotics around the clock. I was given prophylactic medication in large doses to clean up the infection that seeped through my system when the pituitary abscess was pierced by the surgeon's knife. Almost every day the phlebotomist came to take blood from me, or to start the IV in a different vein. I soon became two weeks post op. The doctors in attendance from the Surgical and E.N.T. Dept; trooped in and out of my room smiling, and rattling off to each other the details and progress of my surgery.

Soon the I.V. Nurses were unable to find any good veins to give me my antibiotics through. They poked and prodded up and down the avenues of both my arms, but all veins were collapsing. What to do next! I really needed this IV therapy. My medication was held for twenty-four hours, and I thought maybe I didn't need it any more.

The doctors still came in to see me, calling out my name as they came near my bed. Each one baring good news. One stated "Mrs. Green do you know, you're a success story, I answered back quickly, "Thanks be to God, I'm a miracle walking." At this time I was up in the morning, caring for my daily toiletry, so you see I was doing all the unexpected. I had no pain and my vital signs were stable. I had survived two very serious brain operations, and all within three months.

Most of the doctors were interns, rookies in their craft, eager to put their book learning to practice. "And how are you feeling?" each one would enquire. "No pain at all?" They hoped I would agree and I did, for I had no pain at all, in any part of my head. Now they stood outside my room in a whispering circle, discussing me as usual. I saw them glance over at my bed. Finally two doctors came back in again and talked to me in very hushed tones.

"You have no more accessible veins, Mrs. Green, we have to find another port for your medication. I being a nurse was alerted at this time. Were they considering a "Cut down."? No that could not be for me. I had assisted in many such procedure at bedside. They, understanding my questioning mind, said "No Mrs. Green not a cut down; but something relatively new and much safer. "We can place a Hickman Catheter in your right chest vein, which has to be done under sterile surroundings. My eyes widen, "Back to the OR again? I asked. The doctor speaking nodded and patted my hand. "Yes its a very simple procedure, but safe and you will not feel it once its inserted, and we will have a vein for your medication without having to search and continue to prick you. "We will speak to the surgical resident and he will come to speak to you." The date was set for me to go back to the OR almost immediately. I talked with the children and they understood that it was imperative that my medication therapy be not interrupted.

This was another challenge. Another chance to wholly trust in God. I had no other choice. I was tired and weary of being sick. I longed for release, to be free of the net I felt trapped in. I dreaded the IV. Nurses who roamed the floors every day with their silvery trucks looking for their next victim. God is Good. He was good to me. The procedure was done and finished in less than two hours, and I felt only the pricking of the surgeons' stitches as he finished the job.

That night, the same night of the day of the insertion of the Hickman catheter in my right Vena Carva, I became ill. I was in deep sleep, but they're suddenly possessed my right chest where the catheter was inserted a deep hot searing pain. It was like a hot knife turning and twisting inside of me. My bladder was full, but I did not recognize the need to pass my urine, because of the pain in my chest.

Despite the fact that the veins in both my arms had collapsed, the doctors in the OR had found a vein in my left arm to receive the anesthesia needed for the procedure. Now in the night, the IV had infiltrated, and the area around the needle was swollen and painful. I felt I was drowning in deep icy cold waters. I was not fully awake, but I knew I was calling out loudly and groaning. I felt myself to be sinking. Suddenly I felt two soft warm hands, holding onto my left hand, caressing it, and a soft quiet voice repeating the 23rd Psalm. I learned later it was my roommate, the young lady Myra Dugan in the bed by the window. We had repeated the 23rd Psalm together in our short encounter together to comfort each other. I felt she had more problems than I, both physical and emotional. Here she saw me in my distress and called on my God to come to my aid. I don't know whether she knew him as personally as I did, but she knew the God that I served. Soon the Nurses arrived, pulled me back up in my bed because I was almost over the rails in agony. I soon became quiet and peaceful as her sweet soft voice crooned those comforting words that she told me she knew in our earlier conversations. She also sang to me "Yes Jesus

Loves Me, she sang it over and over again, velvety and soft like, watching me through her bedrails, and her fingers barely touching mine. A nurse gave me an injection, covered me, and hung around my room until she heard my even breaths of sleep.

From that moment on I felt the loving arms of my Savior Jesus Christ enfolding me close to his bosom. I learned about my dear Savior during my early childhood days. I tried to live a Christian Life according to His precepts and commandments. I knew Jesus Christ as my personal Savior, who died on the cross to save me from my sins, and is now my soon coming King; but I don't think I have ever felt him any dearer or nearer to me as He was that night. I will never forget the sweet presence of His Holy Spirit as he calmed me and soothed me using the voice of that dear young lady in the bed next to mine.

In the morning I was weary, but I felt a peaceful calm about me. Many doctors came to see me that morning. They inspected the wound around the catheter insertion, and reassured me that all was well. I had survived a third surgical procedure, although this one, not as serious as the first two. My antibiotic therapy was now resumed using the new port through the Hickman Catheter. Twelve inches of the catheter remained on the outside of my body with a clamp on the end of the tubing used to open for receiving the medications and to close when the infusion was finished. I seriously needed the medication to cleanse out my system from the ruptured abscess that my little glandular friend Pettie Terrie (Pituitary) was holding.

I was out of bed following day, very weak at first, going to the bathroom, but Thank God definitely on the mend. My room friend Myra Dugan and I had some extended conversations, and I and my two daughters, Valerie and Edie were able to witness to her about the saving grace of our Lord Jesus Christ, and she was very receptive. I was scheduled to receive at least six weeks of around the clock therapy. I had already received two weeks of medication before my veins collapsed. The doctors were conferring with each other, visiting me each day, and telling me what great progress I was making; but I never let any of them forget that my God was the Chief Consultant on my case.

Soon the day arrived for the Hickman Catheter to be removed from the large Ven Carva vein in my right chest that conveys blood to the right atrium of the heart. I began to feel a little scary now. This was to be another trip back to the operating room, for it had to be removed under sterile conditions. The doctors and Nurses advised me that it was no big thing. So I contented; left myself in the hands of the

Lord. I felt that God had not brought me thus for to leave me.

Prior to this event I had begun to see figures and shapes more distinctly now. The doctors would hold up two or three fingers, and ask how many did I see. But the real test came when I could distinguish the difference between a one, five, ten, or twenty-dollar bill. I could now see both eyes on my children and not just the jewelry they were wearing. Praise God! The shadows were beginning to flee. I felt a deep joy overflowing my spirit. I always knew God was a healer, but looking in the mirror on the day of my final discharge from the Hospital, I saw the faint visage of a walking miracle.

I am home now with my family as I recover from the two very serious brain operations and two minor ones with the insertion and removal of the Hickman Catheter. Shall I count the pocket of flesh removed from my left lower abdomen used to wall off my brain from my sinus cavity? Yes five procedures in all of the first six months of 1993. My legs are a little weak at times, I cannot move as fast as I used to and I am on a lot of oral medications, but my sight is becoming clearer everyday. I had gained a new vision now; a spiritual insight. Everyone now, no matter who is my neighbor, and you know we are commanded to love our neighbor as we love ourselves. Sometimes this is just a catch phrase with a lot of us, but a neighbor is anyone near or far and sometimes with a need. Did not the "Good Samaritan" in the bible care for the victim who had fallen prey to the robbers? When my sight was shadowy I learned new perceptions. The tone or lilt of a speaking voice imparted the true inner feelings of the speaker. The crisp quick footsteps of my daughter coming down the corridor told me that she was eager to visit me. I listened to the birds chirping outside my window, and the bird mates calling back to each other. I never enjoyed a cool slice of watermelon as much as I did that day I was allowed liquids after my first surgery. My family always ate this ambrosiatic fruit of peasants and royalty, but I used to begrudge the fare of watermelon because of the disposal of it rinds and seeds. But now I experienced and enjoyed its cool satiny taste and was thankful.

The new smells, oh how exhilarating! Suddenly I recognized new and fresh odors. Plants and flowers, a fresh cup of tea, all were new scents to me. Oh how wonderful our God is. Not only is He great and good, but also He is aware of the needs of his children. So God said, "Until the Shadows flee away," I will intensify all my dear ones senses. The Shadows are lifting now. I am seeing better now through the windows of my soul I thank God for the experience of this affliction. I don't revel in it and I try to forget all the real hard places in the midnight hours, but I will never forget how my Savior Jesus Christ was with me through the shadows. Now the motif in my Tapestry is so much clearer and intense now because the dark colored ribbons do intensify the brighter colored ones in the Tapestry of my life.

CHAPTER TWENTY

Sitting In My Own Tent Door

The sun is setting, going down slowly behind the rooftops. Yes, my skyline is a number of smoky rooftops, jutting out, one behind the other, and I am sitting here in my own tent door. My tent door is the entrance into the spirit of my soul. I sit here quietly, thinking and wondering. I think of all the things that have happened to me in my short pilgrimage here on this planet Earth.

Yes the spirit of my soul is a tent, and I am sitting in my own tent door. All the props and hampering of my life are gone and I am left alone now with the Tapestry of my life spread out before me.

In actuality, I am in my little apartment on the fifth floor, furnished with all the do-dads and the trappings that my children have lavished on me. Some things not used or needed, but are representative of their love and care for me. I do feel comfortable warm and cared for. The long list of telephone numbers on my kitchen wall directory attested to the loving communications that come into me during the week. "Mommy, are you alright?" "Do you have any pain?" "Mommy do you need anything from the store?" They call me Mommy but I feel that sometimes we are playing reverse roles. The children are the parents and I am the child. Each one of my children feels that I must be obedient to their wishes and commands. To keep well, stay warm, not to catch cold, not be lonely. You name it and this is their concern. I look back and I think to myself, "How did Sam and I raise five children, and these same five have such a hard time raising me into senior hood. This is the whole problem, adult children have a hard time swallowing the idea that Mom and Dad if they live long enough, will grow older, become slower, forgetful and sometimes even a little crabby.

I continue to wonder, why can't we be left to be what we really are as nature and time designate for us. Why should we try hard when we are sixty, seventy or more to revert back to being thirty or forty? That's what adult children really want. They do not want to see their parent's age, but we do not expect a two year old to act any different than a two year old. He must always say No! No! When requested to do anything. He must touch everything he sees, and waddle around the furniture on unsteady fat legs until he loses his balance and goes boom on the floor. We then run and grab the two year old kiss his fat little cheek and watch him try again.

The teenager must be a teenager, learning and trying out new experiences, of course within certain limitations. He or she will get excited over a first or new date. A new car, or the first driving lessons will be overwhelming. They must squeal with delight and jump about for joy. These are their teen years. I am now in my senior years, and I am enjoying them immensely. I love being alone and quiet to myself. Sometimes the phone rings and I let it ring, I know sometimes this is very unfair when the person at the other end of the phone simply wants to know if I am alright. I answer the phone without picking it up. Yes I'm home, have been in all day. No I didn't go out for a walk. Mommy, you didn't walk today? How come? Remember I told you, you must walk everyday? "Well today was my think day." I just wanted to stay home and think. Long pause. Think about what, Mommy? What in the world do you have to think about? Oh you sweet dear, I would reply to the silent phone. If it were just you I thought about, it would be worlds of thought.

Sometimes I think of Sam, my poor dear other half. At the time of this writing we have been married forty-five years. We are not together living under the same roof, but I can truly attest to this fact that we feel closer to each other and more aware of each other's needs than when we were both under the same roof. But a lot of sorry circumstances, stubbornness on both of our sides, ill health, separated our dwellings. But we communicate as frequently as we possible can. We compare notes about our adult children, and comfort each other verbally and emotionally. We both have made mistakes in this life we are aware of them and realize that some are irreversible. But thanks be to God, all our shortcomings, and sins are covered by the Blood of Jesus Christ our Savior and are thrown in the depths of the sea of his forgiveness to be remembered no more.

You will not always find me sitting in my tent door. Sometimes I walk about inside my tent. This occurs when I take my precious Bible in hand and turn from page to page, reading and allowing the Holy Spirit to anoint my soul and enlighten my mind. My first recollection of the phrase to sit in your own tent door was when I was a little girl and my mother would take Jean and I to Sunday night service. Our

Minister would always make the statement before starting his Sermon. Everyone sit quietly in your own tent door.

I remember vividly one Sunday night Sermon in particular. It had been a warm Sunday and most of the less then one hundred worshipers that had gathered in the church that evening were sluggish, from eating their Sunday fare of fried chicken or roast port chops and potato salad. Most of them had attended morning service at 11am followed by 1pm Sunday school. Some of the young sisters had sleeping babies on their shoulders. The front now with the elder deacons, eyes half closing down were very quiet while our dear Minister labored with his sermon and with little response from the congregation. Sprinkled in amongst the worshipers were a handful of young people. I was not old enough at the time to be included in. They were neither asleep nor awake. But as I clearly remember they were eyeing one another, and waiting for service to be over so that they could gather with each other outside in the warm August night and separate into pairs walking home. The Mothers, mine included, wiped their brows, fanned themselves and watched the clock on the wall. There were a few Amen's verbalized now and then when the Minister raised his voice. But there was something wrong here. He sensed it in his spirit as he looked over his audience. He saw before him a large auditorium with seating for at least five hundred people. He saw the empty seats turned up, as if no one was expected to sit in them. He felt the lethargy in their spirit. No one was sitting in his or her tent door listening to the word of God coming from his messenger.

My dear sweet quiet Rev. Ellison became moved by the Holy Spirit, gave one loud cry in a deep commanding voice. Church! Church! Wake up, you are not sitting in your own tent door," You are all off in dreamland somewhere." He called again church, in a loud demanding voice, made one high leap over the side of the podium and ran around the church crying loudly. "Why are these chairs empty, shoving them down and up again. Why are these chairs empty? Why are you people sleeping? Wake up church! Wake up church! And sit in your own tent door. I dare say, no one ever showed signs of weariness or lethargy again while in a Sunday night worship service, and I understood instantaneously the meaning of the phrase Sitting in your own Tent Door.

This is also inventory time. Time to take stock of the condition of yourself and your own soul's salvation. No time to point fingers at others. No time to blame. President Truman had a plaque on his desk "The Buck stops Here; we must realize that we are responsible for all our commitments and the outcome of the same.

The spirit of my soul is not cluttered anymore. All the extra baggage I had been dragging around with me for years, I have finally dropped off. Old raggedy stuff I thought could be repaired and used again has been wrapped up tied up and discarded. The stuff of fear, discouraged rags of loneliness and despair also wrapped together and thrown out together.

I have a new song to sing. The song of the Redeemed. I am redeemed by the Blood of the Lamb. The Lamb being Christ my Savior. I found him when I was a little girl. I thought I knew him altogether well. He proved himself to me when I was attending high school and he kept me then from the wiles of the devil that was prevalent back in those days. From the nineteen forties to the fifties was during my early adult days, and God protected me then as he does now.

He was my divine guidance when raising my family. Those hard days when I had not the answers to my children queries; I had to fall on my knees and place my petitions before a great God who has all the answers, knows the beginning from the end and who holds the whole world in His Hand.

Sitting here reminiscing alone, in the quiet of the spirit of my soul, I look back and beyond memory. Before time began. Before worlds and galaxies were thrown in place; the great creator of these independent star systems knew of me. Not only did He know me but also He was aware of my current needs. Isn't this thought mind boggling? Yes! It is to me. From the time of my earliest recall, I was aware of the hand of God on my life.

I see in the faint sketches of mind, probably no older than three or four a little girl jerking free of her mother's hand and jumping in back of a Lexington Ave Trolley Cable car between 100 and 101st Street. I was not maimed or injured. The vehicle came an eighth of an inch from touching me.

I remember another little girl maybe five or six years old screaming, Mama, Mama! Wake up! Mama was sprawled out on the dusty pavements on 86th Street and Madison Ave in front of a drug store where Mama had just stepped in to buy some medicine for her terrible headache. I did not know what happened to Mama. I know now that Jeanie and I was left to the mercies of the passers' by who called the "Hospital truck" as we called it back then. Lucky back then a Doctor usually accompanied the Ambulance when making their rounds. I heard the words "heat stroke," "skin as red as a beet," and I do remember it being a very hot day and Momma promising Jean and I a penny icy as soon as she bought her medicine.

I also remember poor Daddy being beat to a pulp, his nose broken his ears boxed in, his scalp cut open by three Italian thugs, as they were called by the police looking for money and jewelry. When Daddy refused and put up a feeble retaliation, they dragged him limply behind some trashcans in an alleyway between Stebbins Ave and Prospect Ave to bleed to death and die. But my Great God at this point reversed the circumstances. He saw little me, needing her Daddy at such a tender age of five years. He woke up a sweet little old lady who thought she heard some cats disrupting her nicely stocked trash cans under her window and she did not think 10PM was too late for her to go out and investigate. Surely she did not expect to find what she did see. A sadly beat up man groaning now, "Please help me," "Please take me home." She thought at first he was a drunk, a vagabond, these were the depression days, and many men, young and old had given up on life and became derelicts. But as she timidly took a closer look, she saw that he was a dapper man, dressed in suit and tie, and speaking softly. "Please lady take me home." As Daddy told the story to us afterwards of how this little old lady pulled him up to a sitting position, and went to the corner police call box and put in a call for the police. They came with little delay and took him to the hospital. Daddy was walking home from church that night which he then attended in the Bronx that night straight into Manhattan as he often did to save a nickel trolley ride. He often walked this distance and stated he could do it in one half hours time.

Mama watched for him that night. She checked the windows and the peephole in our front door. Listened for any voices behind the stairwell. We had no telephone in those days. She would have to wait for morning light to call the police to let them know that Charlie did not come home as he was expected to. He never was out after 11 PM, even when the service was long and high.

Mama waited, watched and prayed. Little as I was, I felt her anxiety, and I said my little innocent prayers which God soon answered. Mama rocked me in her arms crooning "Yes Jesus Loves Me," I know now, not to sooth me, but for her comfort.

We might have both been dropping off to sleep when about 5 AM in the morning we both heard a distinct Rap-Rap-Rap on our front door. We had no doorbell then. The shrill voice came loud and clear. "Police Open Up." "Police open up." I know Mama's heart was racing, I could tell by the way her hands were beating at her chest. But behind the Police's voice, I heard my Daddy's voice calling out faintly. Joey, it's me, you can open up. Joey it's me, I'm all right.

The police had taken my Daddy to the Hospital. They had cleaned his wounds and stitched his head. There was nothing they could do for his broken nose but let it repair itself because his nose certainly was not going anywhere. Daddy had a very high bridge bone any way for a nose; and years later he would always make jest of his nose, saying nothing unsavory would escape his smellers.

On another occasion, not as late, most likely in the afternoon, Mama and I were coming home from a shopping trip on 1st Ave, where you could buy all the fruits and vegetables that you wanted at half price, because there was no middle man. When the three of us Mama, Jeanie and I got back into the apartment, Mama noticed her bedroom window leading to the fire escape was half way up. She knew she did not leave it that way. Someone knew we were not at home. Someone planned to come in and go through the drawers of the furniture, looking for money and jewels. Everyone in those days had some kind of jewelry left over from their family's heirlooms. "Mothers" rings or pearls were precious, and the only link between a much earlier affluent era.

There was a long crowbar lying on the windowsill. Pair of sturdy brown boots was standing on the steps of the fire escape. The perpetrator was not sure whether he was discovered, so he remained perfectly still, figuring out his next move.

Mama grabbed the two of us and through us behind the kitchen door, and told us "Don't move, don't make a sound and pray." This was not hard for Jeanie and I to do; we had often played these games, but for some reason we knew this was for real. Mama quickly and quietly pulled out Daddy's tool chest under the large cupboard in the corner of the kitchen. She grabbed his long handled hatchet that Daddy sometimes used to chop off his fresh feathered chicken heads and hid it behind her long skirts. Jeanie and I both peeked between the crack of the door where we could see past the living room and straight into Mama's bedroom.

Suddenly Mama was banging and banging on those sturdy brown boots, chopping and screaming as she did so

In the Name of Jesus, In the Name of Jesus of Jesus she cried. Chop! Chop! May you never walk again! She caught him off balance, and he almost went over the rails as she told us later. He had no chance to reach for the crow bar that he used to break the lock and pry open the window.

She banged on his ankles a few more times, and shouted up to him. "I hope I brake your bunions." Now go home to your Mama. She quickly shut tight the window, pulled down the shades, and worried how to secure the window until Daddy came home from work, since the lock was broken.

Jeanie and I laughed and romped on the couch imitating the same scene over and over again. This would be another new game for us to play together, the burglar game. Mama was spent as she sprawled out on the corner of the couch. She had no strength left to stop our revelry and romping. She wiped her face, and moaned to herself over and over again, "Thank God," "Thank God" he's gone. I don't think he'll ever come back here again.

Soon Daddy came home for supper, that Mama managed to throw together as she said. When Daddy heard the story he laughed at first and kissed Mama and told her how brave she was.

When we were sleeping that night, Daddy had found some narrow planks that he nailed across the lower part of the window. He opened the window "just a smidgen" he said, and he opened the transom over the bedroom door to afford more ventilation. "Now sleep," he said. Lets sleep, Gods watching over us.

Jeanie was already asleep, I could hear her light breathing next to me. My lids were heavy. I wondered to myself, Mama must somehow be related to God. She always called on him in any and every crises, as I could remember.

Born in the Bronx, my early days spent on the "Avenues." Moved to Manhattan, all during the depression days. Back up in the Bronx again with Daddy and Mommy keeping their family together during the Post War days, Adolescent, and early adult days all spent surrounded by the love and care of my family.

But my story is deep, deep as the ocean and wider than all the seas in the world.

Words in all the books of the world could not tell it all. The ways of Gods' Love and care cannot be explained without the knowledge of who He is. But my trembling lips can but whisper in the quiet of the night. He is Jesus Christ the Savior of the world; the obedient Son of God who gave his life for the sins of all those who would believe on him and dare to live according to his precepts through faith and his grace. I am not a preacher, neither seer, nor teacher. But my soul is a witness for my Lord. He is the Good Shepherd leading me through green pastures everyday with his staff to keep me close and not to stray. He is Living waters, after which taking the first drink, one will never thirst again. He is the Bread of Heaven, not as that manner which came down from heaven as in the wilderness. But the staff of life for he has truly been my satisfying portion. What more can I say? The sun is going down over the rooftops, and I am warm and comforted sitting in the Tent door of my soul.

CHAPTER TWENTY-ONE

The Finished Product

My dear friends I have a secret to share with whoever wants to take a few moments and read further on. The secret some may know already. So this is not a closed secret, but one that anyone can know, if their hearts and minds are open to spiritual adventure.

We know that in the beginning was God! We know and understand this fact from one of the greatest references known to mankind throughout the world, the Holy Bible. Here in the Holy Scriptures we meet God on the first day known to our existence. Not God's first day, because He always was. But it was in this instance that He began to reveal himself to mankind.

In this first day, God made light and darkness divided the two from each other and he called the evening and the morning the first day. God continued to create from day one to day six. The great mastermind of the universe caused great and small stars to shine by night and day. Great bodies of water to ebb and flow upon the created land. The fowls in the air, the fish in the sea, and every creeping animal, insect or swimming fish, great or minute is evidence of His great and majestic powers.

When He came to man, God outdid himself because He created us in His own image. As startling as it may seem to some poor sin beleaguered persons, we mankind, traveling through this vale of tears bare the image of God.

Is this the secret? No this is not the secret that I would unveil to you. Maybe some of my patient readers already know the secret. Many of us and most everyone in the deep recesses of their souls want to believe that they were created in the image of God. No one wants really to believe that they evolved from a monkey no matter how cute he maybe all dolled up in a circus suit. There is a yearning in the souls of men to truly know how they and their ancestors arrived on this planet and with what powers did it all come about. The Bible tells it all. The Bible reveals the whole truth of man.

His very instant being created from the dust of the ground in the first book of Genesis. But this is not what I want to impart. This is not my secret. Also, my secret will not be a secret, if you will but take the time out everyday and read the Holy Scriptures; starting from Genesis straight on through until you reach the book of The Revelations. Be patient with yourself, use a King James Concordance, and take your time reading through the Old Testament and Psalms, Proverbs, skipping over nothing. It most likely may take you a year or two to finish the whole Bible. Read it prayerfully, and ask God the Holy Spirit to illuminate the pages.

I know that this will be a very tedious task for anyone, who does not like to read, for the very harassed young mother with little ones to care for everyday. But for no matter who reads my simple words, this is a challenge. It will be an extraordinary experience and you will be blessed in doing so.

Now I have not forgotten my secret that I want to impart. Maybe by the time you have finished reading the Bible, the secret will reveal itself to you. But for those who have never gone through the Holy Scriptures at such lengths, it might take too long to get to the revelation of the secret. And my dear friends time is too short. Time my dear friends is winding down. God is soon to return to this planet Earth. It may be anytime now, or before this century is out. No one knows the exact time of this great event. Only God the Father knows when Jesus the Son will come back to this Earth to gather his loved ones to himself from the four corners of the world.

I am coming to my secret now. It is simply this. God is not finished with us yet. We may be cast down, cast about; brow beaten, physically or mentally impaired, but God is a God of second chances. He did not shut up the books of judgment, shake his head and dust off his hands when our first ancestors sinned by disobedience in the Garden of Eden and walk away from it all. Did you know this? Do you realize that when you look in the mirror every day, you do not see the finished product? No my dear friends what you see is not what God intended you to see or be. He had great expectations for man. That is why He prepared him a beautiful habitat, the Garden of Eden for Adam and Eve before he created them. They were perfect in every way, in knowledge, beauty, and strength until the Serpent beguiled them and they fell from Gods graces and were cast out from their beautiful home, the Garden of Eden. Thereafter the man had to till the ground and toil daily by the sweat of his brow to eat his bread. The woman's part was pain and travail in birth. The ultimate punishment was death because they disobeyed God when they ate of the forbidden fruit of the Tree of the Knowledge of Good and Evil. He had to pronounce death on them at this point and drive them from this beautiful paradise where the Tree of Life was. If they had not taken the fruit of that tree then they would be living forever in their sins.

But God had no intentions of death for his creation, but he could not let them continue in their sins. But God in his infinite wisdom knew what would transpire, knew that Man would fall and made provisions for their salvation. When our Great God, looked upon fallen man His heart was broken and grieved. But God The Father, God The Son and God The Holy Ghost had already had a Summit Meeting before the Foundation of the World, and it was already ordained that Jesus, God the Son would leave the Ivory Palaces where he dwelt in glorified splendor along side his Father; and come down to the Beggarly elements of this terrain and shed his blood for the redemption of all those who would believe on him, surrender their lives over to him, live love and honor him by the grace that He would empower them to do so.

So now when you look in the mirror everyday, look not at just what that shadowy glass is telling you, but look beyond your image and see by faith the person God intended you to be. By the revelation of his Holy Word and the atonement of His precious blood applied to your heart and soul and the faith that God will give you to believe, you can be saved. Yes saved in body soul and spirit and you can be changed.

No one needs to walk around unhappy and distraught with his or her spiritual plight. God is still on His Throne. He is not finished with mankind yet. What you see in the mirror is not the finished product. The time between the falls of man in the Garden of Eden up until this present time is but a moment's sigh with God. God does not regard time as we do. We may get weary and tired waiting for situations to change. Eons of time have come and gone, but God's ways are changeless and past finding out. Jesus is now waiting on the edge of eternity for the signal from God the Father to determine the end of time. Then and only then will there be no more time to get in readiness for the greatest event of all the ages. This will be the return of Jesus Christ the King to this sin encumbered earth to gather his bride unto himself; which are all those who have placed their lives wholly in his hands to change and mold as he would. At that moment all those who have accepted Him as their personal savior and lived their lives according to His will and gentle pleading, with the help of his love and grace will be changed. Changed in a moment quicker than an eye twinkle. God is getting his people ready now for that big change. Read the sign posts along the way. Observe the political storm clouds. Read your Bible, and be also ready for you do not know when the Son of Man will return to this earth to claim his bride. For Jesus Christ is the Bridegroom, and we are His Bride The Finished Product.

CHAPTER TWENTY-TWO

The Parade Story

My story is not finished yet. I can't seem to wrap it up and put it to bed. I think I will tell a little bit more about my father, Charles Jennings Ratteray. I sometimes wonder about him. A quiet spoken man, God fearing, self taught, punctual and with a sense of humor and many wise sayings. He once said to me many years ago, that God gave me two ears and one mouth with a good purpose in mind. He wanted me to listen twice as much before I spoke once. He was born in Hamilton Bermuda in 1896. This makes him ninety-seven years at this writing. Bermuda is a self governing British Colony located in the Atlantic Ocean, east of Cape Hatteras. It is a beautiful, mild climate, charming piece of vegetation. Here young Charlie loved his native land Bermuda. He enjoyed his boyhood along with his other brothers and sisters which were seven surviving ones out of thirteen births.

My mother also was from a large family of sixteen children, also of which seven survived. She also a native of that tiny Island of Bermuda. As a little girl she ran and romped with her siblings playing and growing up as any normal child. They emerged and matured in the early years of the 20th century when new change and progress were in vogue.

That tiny piece of greenery had nothing to offer the natives. It was a dreamland for tourists and Honeymooners. In those early years, and up until the war years, there came a great influx of native Bermudians to the States.

My Mama and Daddy having met and married arrived also in the 1920's. Mama came first and Daddy arrived a year later, and both worked in service, Mama as a cook and Daddy as a chauffeur and Valet' man. There first stop was Canada, then down into the state of Connecticut, then into the State of New York.

I often wondered to myself, how does it feel to live on this earth so long. Daddy has lived out ninety-seven years, and when I asked him his secret, he told me with his sheepish grin, "just keep your mouth shut and your bowels open." Well this really tickled my funny bones. Daddy was a man of a few words and when he spoke them they were either words of wisdom or words full of mirth.

I sang Happy Birthday over the phone for him this morning and asked the same question. I knew Daddy was about to say something profound. "Yes Daddy," I said, "how does longevity come about?" "Well", he said clearing his throat as usual. "You cannot start at the end of life, you have to start at the beginning. "Yes I know," I said, everything should start at the beginning." "But what Daddy," "start what?" I knew what he was going to say; at least I thought I knew. Live right; treat your fellow man right, etc, etc. But this was not the case this morning.

"Muriel dear" he continued very slowly and quietly measuring his words always careful not to offend. "My Papa, your Grandfather taught me in the early days to honor, respect and obey my elders." "I did this to the best of my ability and it has paid off in long life."

"But Daddy, you left home as a very young man."

"Yes I did my dear, and until I left I followed rules of the home." "When I came to the States I never forgot the precepts that were laid out to me." Then he paused again. "Do you remember the Parade Story?" "Yes I do I laughed." That was a cute story." "No my dear, it was not cute, it was a reality; and I can remember the quick whacks of my fathers' walking stick even now, that one time I deliberately disobeyed him." We talked only a few minutes more; I sent love to him over the wires and hung up. Daddy was not a longwinded person, over the telephone or otherwise.

I sat for a moment and wondered. The Parade Story came back to me as he had told it years ago to Jeanie and I when we were little girls.

It seemed that Daddy was a young energetic lad of nine years of age. Daddy and his family lived on Front Street in Hamilton, Bermuda. Daddy's father was a robust stocky man, always carrying a walking stick, which served his person well, allowing the children to realize he was close at hand by his tapping on the front porch steps. Papa Ratteray had a strong booming voice that bounced off the walls of his Parish church every Sunday morning. The rest of the children knew not to disobey Papa, especially when it came to the West Indian Parade that was to come down Front Street one Saturday morning. He had left orders for no one to go out or run after those loud raucous music makers.

It appeared that young Charlie had forgotten his father's admonishing words. I don't know what the other children were doing, or the whereabouts of Mama and

Papa on that Saturday morning in question, but I do know as it was recalled to me, that young Charlie could not resist the beating of the drums, the humming of the horns and stringed instruments. He got himself dressed and out of the house and up the street to where the parade was tuning up.

I don't know how or when he was discovered, but he was discovered to be in the wrong place at the wrong time. The Rev. Ratteray reached for his black preacher's hat and trusty walking stick and went out looking for his son. He realized now that the humming beat of the music would be more than Charlie could resist. Having found his presence absent early that morning he went searching for him. There he was, found where he thought he would be, right at the beginning of the Parade.

Papa gently guided him with his walking stick away from the crowd and when he was in sight of his house and siblings, he taught him his much needed lesson in obedience. Daddy stated he never forgot that incident and as long as he remained under his father's roof, he was governed by the rules and regulations of the home. When he arrived in the States, he never forgot his father's loud booming voice from the pulpit and those quick stinging swipes he received from his father's walking stick and these memories kept him in line all these many years.

Dear Daddy, I thought to myself. There is a depth in all that you have said to me, for what your father taught you, you have imparted to me, each in your own unique way.

At this writing, I have five adult children and a very intelligent young grandson, Glen Jr., eleven years old. I have not been blessed with many grandchildren and may not have any others, but I can truly say that my children and grandson have been a blessing to me. I don't know if I have always been an obedient daughter in my younger years or an honoring daughter in my adult years which give rise to longevity but I am striving every day to walk the straight and narrow paths that eventually lead to our heavenly home above. No matter what the number of days for me may be I just want to run this race with diligence and pass the baton on to the following generations who are now keeping pace besides me. When I am ready to pass it, or it falls from my hand, they will quickly grab it and burst on speedily to the finish line.

Obedience to God, His will and His way; Honor to our forefathers who have gone before us is part of the ingredients that make up the stuff that's leads to long life. Let's not be caught up in the parade that's coming down the street. The beat is catchy and the costumes and floats are bright. But what is the message of the moment? The parade will soon be over. The participants will be tired and go home. The little lad was not punished because he went to the parade but because he disobeyed his father.

The world is changing. It has drastically changed since the turn of the century. But the old rules and landmarks have the same meaning and the full circle has almost completed itself. Hopefully we will not have to cook meals on wood and coal stoves ever again, unless we are camping out in the woods. I don't believe we ladies will have to drape ourselves in heavy head shawls and lace ourselves up in tight corsets as our great grandmothers did, but we must search in our cabinets; on the top shelves of our book cases, take down the old leather Bible, blow off the dust and go through those precious pages. Here find answers to the problems of the ages. I have stated this before in my earlier chapters. Our country was founded on the Standards found in the Holy Bible. Our trust has been in God, This we have printed on our money exchange. IN GOD WE TRUST. Our Presidents have taken oaths on their Inauguration Day to defend and protect their country with hands on the Bible.

We cannot let this guide slip away from us. We must continue herein. Our forefathers fought in wars, suffered on foreign battlefields, while those at home prayed us on to victory. The synopsis of all this verbiage is simply this, to live long on the land in which the Lord thy God giveth thee is to Honor thy Father and Mother. Now I will add to this Holy Rule, my healthy helpful hints handed down by my forefathers. Eat plenty of fruits and vegetables drink adequate amounts of water. Get enough exercise and sufficient rest and recreation every day. Smile and be happy and help someone along the way less fortunate than yourself, and lets not be so caught up in the Parade coming down the street with its noisy blare of trumpets and drums because eventually the marchers and followers eventually get tired and go home.

For more information or if you would like to contact the author, you can write to Muriel at the following address:

Muriel Green
C/O Advantage Books
PO Box 160847
Altamonte Springs, FL 32716

To order additional copies of this book or to see a complete list of all **ADVANTAGE BOOKS™** visit our online bookstore at:

www.advbookstore.com

or for orders only call our toll free order number at: 1-888-383-3110

Longwood, Florida, USA

"we bring dreams to life"™
www.advbooks.com

Printed in the United States
200179BV00003B/100-117/A

9 781597 550963